How to Steal a Presidential Election

HOW TO STEAL A PRESIDENTIAL ELECTION

● ● ●

LAWRENCE LESSIG AND
MATTHEW SELIGMAN

Yale
UNIVERSITY PRESS

New Haven and London

Published with assistance from the foundation established in memory of
Calvin Chapin of the Class of 1788, Yale College.

Yale University Press books may be purchased in quantity for
educational, business, or promotional use. For information, please e-mail
sales.press@yale.edu (U.S. office) or sales@yaleup.co.uk (U.K. office).

Set in Gotham and Adobe Garamond types by
Integrated Publishing Solutions.
Printed in the United States of America.

Library of Congress Control Number: 2023942307
ISBN 978-0-300-27079-2 (hardcover : alk. paper)

A catalogue record for this book is available from the British Library.

This paper meets the requirements of ANSI/NISO Z39.48-1992
(Permanence of Paper).

10 9 8 7 6 5 4 3 2 1

To the plaintiffs in *The Electors Cases,*
who did what the Framers expected they would do,
long after the Framers had been forgotten
(Lessig)

To my parents
(Seligman)

Contents

Preface

We write this book at an uncertain moment. We started it in the shadow of January 6, 2021, the most dangerous legal assault on the integrity of a presidential election in our nation's history. Political leaders of both parties voiced nearly unanimous condemnation after the attack. But that consensus quickly faded when polling showed that the Republican base was still with the president. The Senate acquitted Donald Trump in his second impeachment trial. In the months that followed, MAGA Republicans solidified their support for Trump and the lie that the election of 2020 was stolen from him. The partisan calcification that has plagued our politics over the past decades relegated the violent invasion of the Capitol to "legitimate political discourse" and those criminally prosecuted for perpetrating it to "political prisoners."

As terrifying as that day—and, more important for the purposes of this book, the legal conspiracy leading up to that day—was, we also knew that President Trump and his allies had not even attempted to exploit the most dangerous vulnerabilities in the legal framework in place. The fever hadn't broken. It seemed likely that the worst was yet to come.

Yet in the waning months of 2022, there were glimmers of hope. Some were political. In critical races for governor across the country, voters rejected the most extreme election deniers. Kari Lake in Arizona and Doug Mastriano in Pennsylvania ran on the promise that they would use their power to manipulate the election in 2024. They lost. And in the much more obscure but equally essential races for state secretary of state, not a single prominent MAGA candidate won.

These defeats demonstrate that a critical truth is spreading broadly across America: that democracy is worth defending, and it is worth more than any candidate or any party. For those of us focused obsessively on questions of governance and politics, it seems odd that it would have taken so long for this understanding to spread. Most important, though, the essential truth is that in the end enough Americans care enough about democracy to vote to protect it.

The other source of hope was legal. Against all odds, in its last act of the year and mere weeks before Republicans took control of the House of Representatives, Congress passed a law that makes meaningful progress in protecting presidential elections against precisely the sort of manipulation that threatened in 2020 and that we fear in 2024. The Electoral Count Reform Act was a direct response to those threats, and miraculously eighteen Republican senators defied political condemnation from Trump and his MAGA Republican allies to vote for it. The new law is far from perfect—and we expose its serious remaining vulnerabilities in this book—but it is remarkable that Congress did anything at all.

Yet we are not out of the woods. Even if the norms of a free and fair democracy are reviving and the rules have been strengthened, there is still an enormous threat. That threat may or may not manifest itself in the form of Donald Trump. But the behavior—and the outrages—that Donald Trump inspired are still viable within our democracy. They are still a potentially winning strategy for him or his political heir. And thus, there is more work to be done before we can be confident about our democratic future.

We believe that work begins with the understanding this book offers. The essence of our argument is that the rules as they exist right now—rules given to us by the Constitution, the laws of Congress, and the decisions of the Supreme Court—make stealing a close presidential election possible. How or why can't be conveyed in a tweet. But neither does this story require an advanced degree in law. In the pages that follow, we will sketch the threats that are not really threatening, and the threats that are certain threats, the ones that should keep us up at night. By sketching these threats, our hope is that our body politic might begin to build the immunity it will need to resist anyone who would exploit them.

We are grateful for the help of so many in both thinking through the risks of our current system for electing the president and challenging us on the reforms. We are especially grateful to the students at Harvard who gambled on an uncertain seminar and produced incredibly insightful reflections on the weaknesses of our system, and the reforms. (Their work continues to live at https://ec-faqs.us.) We especially thank Michael L. Rosin, and Jason Harrow, who contributed to the seminar and helped guide the students and our thinking. We are also grateful for the research support by many students, including Abby Baskin, Aidan Calvelli, Justin Gillette, Connor Haaland, Deok Hyun Kim, Kelly Lew, Michael Nanchanatt, Audrey Pope, Tram Tran, and Maddie Zabriskie. Seligman thanks the Campaign Legal Center, particularly Paul Smith and Adav Noti, Ned Foley, Rick Pildes, Rick Hasen, and Jack Goldsmith. We both are endlessly thankful to Sarah Chalfant for bringing this work to Yale University Press.

How to Steal a Presidential Election

A Coup in Search of a Legal Theory

Late on the afternoon of January 4, the plan finally came into view. John Eastman, a law professor and former dean at Chapman University Law School—and former student of Lessig's (in a class that also included Elizabeth Cheney)—had been laying the groundwork for months. Until the very end, few had focused on the details of the strategy or the legal theory behind it. That afternoon in the Oval Office, the key player in Eastman's plan listened as the professor tried to convince him to upend two centuries of American democracy.

Vice President Mike Pence, the argument went, could save the day. The Constitution vested him with the power to decide which votes in the Electoral College should count. Eastman believed that Pence could reject the electors for Joe Biden from Arizona, Georgia, Michigan, New Mexico, Nevada, Pennsylvania, and Wisconsin and instead count the alternative slates of electors from those states for President Trump. That power, Eastman claimed, had been exercised before in the early days of the Republic, when Vice Presidents John Adams and Thomas Jefferson resolved disputes in their own elections for president—disputes that, had they gone the other way, would have denied both the presidency. And, Eastman argued, there was a "very solid" argument that such a power remained. Pence should therefore simply use his constitutional authority to rule President Trump into office. Perhaps the courts would have to sort out whether his theory was right, Eastman conceded, but he thought the Supreme Court would be wary of wading into a "political" dispute.

Most people, when they reflect on what happened on January 6, 2021, find it difficult to view the events as an actual attempted coup. The violence at the Capitol was tragic—five Americans died—but also strangely cartoonish. As actress Lucy Liu put it in Netflix's *Death to 2021,* "It was terrifying and stupid. Like a Muppet reboot of the Vietnam War." No one grounded in reality could have expected that a couple thousand protesters, however violent, could successfully coerce a sufficient majority in Congress—a Congress in which one House was controlled by the Democrats—to reverse their votes and deny Joe Biden his electoral victory. A coerced decision is an invalid decision. And though it would take some weird jurisdictional machinations for the Supreme Court to do so, no doubt the Court would eventually reverse any decision that members of Congress had made with literal guns held to their heads.

Yet reality notwithstanding, the evidence adduced by the January 6 Committee shows that at least some within the White House actually imagined that the threat of force would drive Pence and enough Republicans in Congress to reverse what they knew to be a fair election. And had that happened, who knows where we would be today.

Because the optics would have been very different had Pence followed Eastman's advice. Imagine that, before any violence had erupted, Pence had ruled as Eastman had recommended and counted the Trump electors' votes from enough of the contested states to prevail; imagine that Congress had failed to overrule his decision. In that alternative world, the thousands gathering on the steps of the Capitol would have been cheering rather than rioting. They would have been celebrating, peacefully if passionately, that they had indeed "stop[ped] the steal." The image spread across the globe would have been of masses of people joyfully embracing what they thought was a democracy saved.

January 6 made no sense as protestor-driven violent coup. It would have made perfect sense as the made-for-television confirmation of a legal coup crafted elsewhere.

We were close observers of the events that climaxed on January 6. In July 2020, one of us (Seligman) sent the other (Lessig) an essay about how a presidential election in America could be stolen. Seligman was about to take up a job that would preclude him from publishing the essay. "Is there something you can do with this?" he asked. Lessig answered yes. That summer he petitioned Harvard Law School to teach a seminar with Seligman, titled "Wargaming 2020." The idea of the seminar was to go deep on the legal structure for electing a president in the United States. The central question we would pursue was simple: how could you hack the rules to get a result different from what the election should legitimately yield? In other words, how, using the insanely complex rules given to us in the Constitution and an obscure law enacted almost 150 years ago, could you steal a presidential election?

Over the semester, students poured endless hours into working through that puzzle. Along with Jason Harrow and Michael L. Rosin, we took ten episodes of the podcast *Another Way* to work through every idea they (and we) had for how an election could be hacked. As we got to the end of the season, some of us were genuinely terrified: there was a clear path that people acting in bad faith could take to reverse the results of the election of 2020. Our system, we concluded, was not built to withstand bad faith and willful misrepresentation. As the election approached, we expected both.

Yet we were relieved by how the election ultimately unfolded, at least at first. American democracy had dodged a bullet, or so it seemed, because none of the strategies that we had discovered for subverting the results had been deployed. From November 3, 2020, to January 6, 2021, we grew more confident that nothing untoward was going to happen. We heard rumors of alternative slates of electors meeting and voting. (As you'll see in chapter 5, this was a critical step.) But there was nothing to suggest a coordinated effort to take the measures necessary under the rules as they then existed. A few state lawmakers were complaining, but no state legislature was stepping in to change that state's election's results. Many were hollering. Few were doing anything of real substance.

Then January 6 happened. Neither of us could believe it. Not that there was an effort to reverse the results of a free and fair election— we'd been strategizing about that for months—but that *this* was how they meant to do it. Like almost all Americans, we were shocked and saddened by the loss of life and appalled by the injection of political violence into the seat of our constitutional democracy. Still, the Trump team had picked the dumbest possible strategy for pursuing what we feared they were trying to accomplish. If it was going to happen, we were relieved they did it in a way that was certain to fail.

Yet the most important and haunting revelation was that they were willing to do it at all. That signaled to us that we as a nation needed to think seriously about how to defend against such attempts both in the next election and in every election following that.

This is not a book about January 6, 2021. It is a book about January 6, 2025. Our aim is not to tell the story of what was but to describe the story of what could be. We are, both of us, convinced that the rules as they are—even after the recent amendments to the Electoral Count Act—leave our democracy dangerously undefended. And we believe firmly that an informed and intelligent effort to undermine the results of a close free and fair election could work in America—if the rules governing our presidential elections are not changed.

In this book, we sketch the road map for how those who would seek to defeat our democracy could truly do it—how the legal plot could actually unfold. We describe the steps that would need to be taken to assure a theft of the presidency: what wouldn't work, what might work, and what would certainly work.

In the current political environment, this road map would most likely be used by the Trump wing of the Republican Party—the so-called MAGA Republicans. Yet obviously the legal rules themselves make no reference to one political party or the other. In theory, either party could exploit the vulnerabilities we explore. As the winds of politics change direction, perhaps the Democratic Party might some-day abandon democratic norms in a ruthless pursuit of power. (That, if nothing else, is a good reason for Republicans to want to fix these vulnerabilities as well—if loyalty to democracy and the rule of law alone is not enough.) But as we write in the shadow of January 6, 2021, only one party has shown the shocking willingness to manipu-late the law and to bring us to the precipice of a constitutional crisis.

We are not against the Republican Party. We are certainly not against conservatives. One of us (Lessig) grew up a Republican and was the youngest member of a delegation at the GOP convention in 1980. The other (Seligman) clerked for a Republican-appointed federal judge whom he deeply admires. Both of us cherish friend-ships with people with whom we disagree politically, legally, and phil-osophically.

But we are against the Trump wing of the Republican Party. Watching the slow bending of truth by Republican leaders over the past several years, we accept that this wing may eventually swallow the whole. For our purposes, that does not matter. We are not criti-cizing a substantive political ideology. We are criticizing the aban-donment of shared ideals of a democracy within which ideologies get debated and policies chosen. There are clear examples of Repub-licans who still share these ideals—Mitt Romney, Liz Cheney, Adam

Kinzinger, and others. But there is no blinking the fact that the dominant faction within their party has embraced an ideology that is wholly foreign to the tradition of democracy in America. Cheney and Kinzinger were expelled from the House Republican Caucus, while others, who described those facing criminal charges for violently storming the Capitol as "political prisoners," remained members in good standing. That is the ideology we are criticizing.

This is not to say that Democrats couldn't become the same. They just haven't. If faced with the same incentives, if inspired by a similarly pathological leader, who knows how the party would respond. It is true, but misleading, that Democrats challenged the Electoral College results in 2000 and 2004.[1] It is also true that prominent scholars close to the Democratic Party have recently talked about special powers vested in the vice president—now that the vice president is a Democrat.[2] We have no illusion that one party is inevitably virtue and the other inherently vice.

But we do believe that right now the real threat to our Republic is Red, not Blue. And we believe that if we as a people can be rallied to oppose that threat, we may avoid similar threats in the future, whether Red or Blue.

Some will criticize us as reckless for publishing, as it were, the plans to build democracy's nuclear bomb. We believe that view is grounded in a fundamental mistake. The strategies we describe for exploiting the vulnerabilities in our legal system for electing the president are not state secrets. We hope that by the end of this book they can be understood by lawyers and nonlawyers alike. All we had to do was look. It doesn't take rare genius to understand what's possible or how to execute upon those possibilities. It simply takes motivation, time, and, in our case, a profound fear of the cynical malevolence of those who seek political power. In the frantic rush leading up to January 6, 2021, the Trump team had neither the time nor, apparently, the expertise to plan and execute an effective legal coup. But it would be naive to ignore the risk that many are now working through exactly the strategies we describe here. Unlike us, they plan to use them.

If so, it will not be because we gave them the idea. It will be because our leaders have still failed—though with one important exception that we will discuss in chapters 5 and 6—to act to fix the problems that make this threat so real.

Ignorance and inaction together threaten democracy. We aim to eliminate the former. Too few realize just how vulnerable our system is—at least in a close election, in a world where good faith and a commitment to the norms of democracy are gone. Too little is being done to rally politicians to fix this. What we fear is not that there are people planning to execute this strategy—we're sure there are—but that not enough are rallying to resist it.

And so, our purpose here is to make it clear just what they would do—given the law as it is, and as the Supreme Court has interpreted it, as well as the law as they could make it be. Over seven chapters, we will outline the range of possible strategies. We will describe the likelihood that each of them might be attempted and the risks that each could succeed. Four we believe could not succeed. Three we believe certainly could.

Our hope is that when you see what's possible, you will decide that you don't want to live in a democracy that leaves these possibilities open. There's still a chance that enough of us do want to live in a democracy in which the results of elections are determined by the tally of the votes, not by the manipulation of the law. There is still time for us to act to avoid the disaster these possibilities would create.

At least a little. But time is running short.

2

The Scenario

In normal times, the system for electing the president of the United States—though complex and contradictory and flawed—works fine. Even when stressed, as in the election in 2000 that led to *Bush v. Gore,* it works fine. That's not to say it's a great system. However clever the Electoral College may have seemed in 1787, we both think that time and experience have disproven the political assumptions that led the Framers to adopt it. From the very start it was—and still is—compromised by an antidemocratic structure. But whether you like the system or not, for most of our history, and especially recently, it has worked just fine—at least in the sense that the candidate who legitimately won the most votes in the Electoral College (if not the most votes in the national popular vote) was inaugurated and took office.

Think again about the election in 2000. The final tally in the national popular vote was incredibly close—Al Gore led George W. Bush nationally by 547,398 votes. Yet that national margin was legally irrelevant, and the whole election turned upon just one state: Florida. Its election was even more incredibly close—in the end, the state was called for Bush by just 537 votes. And even that number was ambiguously crafted, with a recount stopped midstream (for internally incoherent reasons), leaving many ultimately unsure about who actually got more votes in the state. (A consortium of national newspapers ultimately hired a "nonpartisan and objective research organization" affiliated with the University of Chicago to examine all the ballots under a range of recount standards. The project concluded that had Florida performed a full recount, Al Gore would have been elected president.)[1]

Despite that uncertainty, and in the face of calls by many to challenge the result, Gore conceded. Shortly after the Supreme Court ruled against him, the vice president gave a nationally televised speech declaring he would not challenge the result any further. Though he had won the national popular vote, and though the process in Florida had been flawed and uncertain—orders of magnitude more uncertain than anything President Trump complained of in 2020—Gore declared that he would respect the result that the Court's decision had determined. "Partisan rancor must now be put aside," he told the nation, "and may God bless [George W. Bush's] stewardship of this country."[2] For the American public, that ended the dispute. History barely noted at the time that Vice President Gore, as president of the Senate, oversaw the counting of electoral votes on January 6, 2001—including the previously contested electoral votes from Florida that handed victory to his opponent. History ignored this detail because Gore didn't try to exploit it.

The plot unfolded very differently in 2020. Despite the total absence of any credible evidence of fraud or manipulation, the Trump campaign waged a massive battle to overturn the results. In the courts, in Congress, on cable news shows, and on social media, the Trump team did everything it could to convince America that Trump had in fact won. In January 2021, the *Washington Post* reported that "70 percent of Republicans said they agreed with President Trump's contention that he received more votes than Joe Biden."[3]

The effort to spread that lie started with an extraordinary propaganda campaign to convince Republicans that Trump had been wronged. It proceeded with intense focus on seven key states. By the end, Trump had lost the litigation battle: sixty-two of sixty-three cases, and the single victory (eventually overturned) earning them a tiny number of votes that would not have come close to changing the result in even one state.[4] Yet with tens of millions of Americans, the former president had won the propaganda war. In late 2021, 46 percent of Republicans told a UMass Amherst poll that Joe Biden was "definitely not" the legitimate president; 71 percent affirmed he was either "definitely not" or "probably not" the legitimate president.[5] The numbers have not improved with time. In May 2023, 68 percent of Republicans said that they think Biden won the presidency "due to fraud," and a majority said that the violence on January 6 was "legitimate protest."[6]

Propaganda alone, however, would not have kept Donald Trump in the White House. To prevail against President Biden, he would have had to successfully press the levers of legal and political power to reverse those states' results. Few in the legal and political establishment thought he could succeed—as an anonymous Republican official mused in the days after the election, "What's the downside for humoring him?"[7] Yet Trump and his allies continued to press the wholly baseless claim that the election had been "stolen." That fight, and those words, led to the bloody insurrection of January 6, 2021.

Our aim is not to relitigate 2020 but to explain the threat that this pattern of resistance creates for 2024. We begin by describing a hypothetical that will set the conditions for each possible intervention described in the balance of the book. It is against the background of this threat that we want the risks we are describing to be understood.

We imagined scenarios like this in the fall of 2020 with our students at Harvard. Yet had we offered this description to the broader public in October 2020, few would have believed it. At the very least, the actual election of 2020 has made such scenarios terrifyingly plausible. And that makes them worth worrying about—not just in a law school seminar but across the United States and with all its citizens.

The first critical assumption in our hypothetical is also the most plausible: that the election in 2024 will be very close. Campaigns, at least well-funded campaigns, have become incredibly good at whittling away the polling differences between two candidates. The closer the results in the next election, the greater the risk of what we describe here. We were saved in 2020 not because the system was strong but because the honest results were so obvious, at least to those who were ultimately responsible for determining the election, whether for or against their own political views. The risk we're describing in this book hangs upon the opposite being the case in 2024: an election whose results are not clear, with plausible stories of fraud or theft coming from either side.

The second assumption we make about 2024 is that the candidates are relevantly similar to those in 2020. That might be Donald Trump versus Joe Biden, but our story does not depend upon it being Donald Trump or Joe Biden. Instead, throughout our story, we will imagine that the race is between a MAGA Republican and a Democrat, though to keep the exposition simple, we'll refer to the Democrat as Biden. Any Democrat works in our story, but only a MAGA Republican makes sense for the concerns we're raising here. Neither of us would support Mitt Romney or Liz Cheney for president. But nothing we're describing would be remotely plausible if either of them were the Republican candidate. This story we're telling turns upon one side being led by someone liberated from truth or the rule of law or any allegiance to democratic norms. Trump demonstrated that he was such a person. Since his rise to power, he has generated an astonishingly large number of imitators. The hypothetical we consider here is that either Trump or one of those imitators is the Republican candidate in 2024.

So, imagine that a MAGA Republican in 2024, like Al Gore in 2000, has received half a million more votes nationwide than Biden. But imagine also that Biden has won enough states to push him to 274 electoral votes—4 more than are necessary to win in the Electoral College.

Now imagine that the vote in many parts of the nation has been marred by claims of fraud and voter intimidation. In anticipation of violence at polling places, election administration officials in key battleground states altered voting and ballot counting procedures to ensure the physical safety of voters and poll workers. Numerous courts have declared those alterations to be illegal, because, according to those courts, the state officials unconstitutionally departed from the election law as written by the state legislatures. The election then turns upon whether the votes affected by those cases are counted.

Even beyond the ballots affected by litigation, partisans supporting Biden—who, again, lost the popular vote—make a concerted effort to insist that the voting was rigged. That Biden "actually" got the most votes nationwide. The MAGA Republican supporters counter that the presidential electors—at least where the law does not require them to cast their ballot in the Electoral College for the candidate to whom they are pledged—should unite the nation by voting for the winner of the popular vote, ignoring their pledge to vote for Biden. Fifteen million Americans sign a petition demanding that the electors take this unprecedented step. It is the largest online petition in the nation's history.

A divided media begins to construct two radically different realities for two wildly polarized audiences. One affirms the victory of the winner of the popular vote, the MAGA Republican—despite the other side's allegations of fraud and corruption. The other affirms the victory of the winner of the Electoral College, Biden—despite the other side's allegations of fraud and corruption. "The rule of the Constitution controls," Democrats insist. "If the presidency went to the winner of the popular vote, we would have campaigned differently." "The people have spoken," the MAGA Republican campaign counters. "We should follow their will."

Everything comes down to the results in one state: North Carolina. Imagine that Biden has narrowly won the popular vote in the state and therefore its votes in the Electoral College. But if the state flipped for the MAGA Republican, s/he would have both the national popular vote and an Electoral College majority on their side. In 2020, North Carolina officials honorably defended the integrity of the state's popular vote. But on January 1, 2025, the current Democratic governor, Roy Cooper, will leave office due to term limits. Imagine that a new Republican governor, loyal to the MAGA Republican candidate for president, is elected in his place. The conflict between the results in the two top races—his own and the race for president—leads the new governor to declare that the results for Biden were "faked." In his first days in office, this new governor vows to do "whatever it takes" to assure that the MAGA Republican is elected to the White House.

As anyone watching closely over the past twenty-five years can recognize, nothing in this hypothetical is politically implausible, because each element has happened already. The two inversions (where the winner in the Electoral College is not the winner of the popular vote) that we've seen in the past twenty-five years benefited Republicans. But we came extremely close in 2004 to seeing an inversion favoring the Democrat. And when Donald Trump thought (incorrectly, as it turned out) that Barack Obama had won the Electoral College in 2012 but that Mitt Romney had carried the national popular vote, he openly called for "revolution."[8] Nothing guarantees that the popular vote will go to the Democrat or that an inversion will favor the Republican. (Nor is this possibility remotely unlikely: in 2022, Republicans received more votes nationally in races for the House of Representatives, but had those votes determined the presidency, Democrats would have won in the Electoral College.)[9] We have also seen allegations, unsupported by any evidence, of widespread fraud; claims of illegality and other irregularities by state officials in the administration of elections; and intense political pressure on state officials, including governors and secretaries of state, to interfere with results. We have also seen insanely close results: Florida in 2000. Our hypothetical therefore hardly takes imagination, because everything in it has already occurred.

So how could this scenario be exploited? What techniques does current law give to either candidate, and what could be added to the arsenal before November 5, 2024, or January 6, 2025?

3

VP Superpowers

Of all the ways that MAGA Republicans might flip the result, the route John Eastman recommended in 2020 is the most certain to fail. Eastman claimed that there was "very solid legal authority" for the view that the vice president had a constitutionally protected power to determine how the electoral votes were cast—and that, in the face of his exercise of that power, "all the Members of Congress can do is watch."

This move would fail in 2025 for two obvious reasons. First, there will not be a Republican vice president in 2025. Thus, whatever special powers the vice president has, they will not be deployed to defeat the election of a Democrat.

Second, and more important for the longer term, there just are no special vice-presidential powers. Contrary to Eastman's claims, the vice president has no constitutional authority in the counting of the electoral votes—except the ministerial duty to "open" the certificates.

It is important to make this second point clearly, because this virus of an idea must be extinguished. There may be a Republican vice president in 2029, or a Democratic vice president might attempt to assert this power. Regrettably, some legal scholars have suggested that Vice President Kamala Harris might "need" to do this in order to counteract Republican election subversion.

So, to incinerate this theory of the vice president's powers forever, we'll first give it some context and then wrap it in a sealed container and launch it into the sun. Even John Eastman may not believe the theory anymore. In an interview on our podcast in October 2021, Eastman said, "Anybody who thinks that that's a viable strategy is crazy."[1] Let's celebrate his belated recognition, even if it doesn't immunize him from accountability for advocating it in the first place. Let's also make sure it sticks.

"Necessity," the saying goes, "is the mother of invention." As Donald Trump's campaign entered December 2020, it was clear that his team needed some invention if they were going to derail what seemed obvious to everyone—that Joe Biden would become the forty-sixth president of the United States on January 20, 2021. Trump and his allies had brought more lawsuits challenging the results of the presidential balloting than any campaign in American history. (That should not be surprising, given that Donald Trump himself was the most litigious person ever to become president in U.S. history. By some estimates, he has been party to more than four thousand lawsuits.)[2]

Those election lawsuits were going nowhere. Court after court dismissed challenges to the process that had led to Joe Biden's victory. Even courts whose judges were appointed by President Trump were unwilling to overrule the clear verdict of the people. Some courts reached those results without reviewing the mythical "evidence" of massive fraud—but that was entirely the fault of Trump and his allies. Sometimes they lacked legal standing to bring the challenges; sometimes they waited until far too late to sue; and sometimes the court ruled that even if Trump's wild conspiracy theories of voter fraud were true, he still wouldn't win. No court ruled that any of Trump's legal challenges could realistically change the outcome in any state, even if the challenge succeeded. In one case, the Trump campaign sued the Philadelphia County Board of Elections, challenging its counting of 8,329 absentee and mail-in ballots that allegedly contained such technical defects as a missing date next to a signature, a missing printed name of the voter, or a missing street address for the voter. The campaign took the case all the way to the Supreme Court, which declined to hear it. Yet even if Trump had won, those 8,329 ballots were far fewer than he needed to overtake Joe Biden, who had won Pennsylvania by more than 80,000 votes.

This is not to say that there weren't moments when it seemed things could have gone differently. The Supreme Court declined to hear any of the cases brought by Trump and his supporters, but a week before Election Day, three justices—Clarence Thomas, Samuel Alito, and Neil Gorsuch—signaled strong support for the "independent state legislature theory" as a basis for reversing state court decisions expanding access to voting amid the pandemic. (We'll return to this doctrine in chapter 7.) And in addition to the Trump campaign's ultimately hopeless court challenges, Texas took the unprecedented legal step of suing Pennsylvania directly in the Supreme Court. (Not surprisingly, the Supreme Court dismissed the case.) But as the year came to an end, it was becoming clear that no court, including the Supreme Court, was going to intervene to save Donald Trump.

As his traditional legal options dwindled to nothing, Trump turned to John Eastman. Eastman reasoned that Vice President Pence should intervene because, Eastman argued, he could.[3]

Eastman's theory rested on one clause of the Constitution. The Twelfth Amendment (as well as the section of the original Constitution that text amended) states: "The President of the Senate shall, in the Presence of the Senate and House of Representatives, open all the Certificates, and the Votes shall then be counted."

Notice something important about the grammar of that clause: it includes both the active and the passive voice. The "President of the Senate" (who is the vice president, when the vice president is in the room, but it refers technically to any presiding officer, regardless of whether he or she is the vice president) is directed to "open all the Certificates." Active voice. But once they are opened, then the "Votes" reflected in those Certificates "shall . . . be counted." Passive voice.

Counted by whom? The Constitution doesn't say. At least not explicitly. Yet from the beginning of the Republic, Congress has always presumed that Congress itself, through its agents, would do the counting. Beginning in 1792, Congress operated under rules that required "tellers" to do the counting. Those tellers were members of Congress, selected by Congress for that specific task. From the start, the tellers have included members of both major parties. From the start, in other words, Congress has structured the procedures for counting electoral votes to ensure fair counting. By giving both sides a chance to review and report on the "Votes," the process guaranteed that any abuse would at least be noticed and that the abused party would have a chance to object to any irregularities.

According to Eastman, that long-standing practice was just wrong. Whether or not Congress had in fact always counted the votes through its own tellers, the Constitution, he argued, vests that counting power in the vice president. And because counting necessarily requires determining the validity of the votes counted, Eastman inferred that the Constitution had vested in the vice president a power to determine whether any "Certificate" is the legitimate certificate that names the real electors.[4] Which means, according to Eastman, that the vice president has a constitutional power to determine that certain electoral votes are invalid and then to count alternative votes in their stead.

On this theory, the Constitution would have vested in Mike Pence the power to decide that the slates of electors from Arizona, Georgia, Michigan, Nevada, New Mexico, Pennsylvania, and Wisconsin were illegal and that alternative slates of "electors" (who had met on December 14, 2020, and voted) were the slates that should be counted instead. That decision would have flipped the election from Joe Biden to Donald Trump—which of course is precisely why Eastman pressed the case as hard as he did.

It's important to understand precisely how radical Eastman's theory of the vice president's powers is. The theory takes the vice president far beyond what the presiding officer of a body typically can do. A presiding officer often makes rulings to help the body's proceedings move along—rulings about who can speak when, whether a motion or objection is carried, and other procedural matters. Critically, those rulings are subject to a vote by the body to overturn them. The majority therefore rules, and the presiding officer's powers are thereby contained. This makes sense in a democracy.

Things are a little more complicated when Congress convenes to count electoral votes, but not in a way that would have mattered in 2021. As two centuries of practice has had it, each chamber would have had to vote separately to overturn the vice president's ruling. If Pence had decided to throw out the votes of a contested state, Congress would have had a chance—in the ordinary case—to overrule him. In 2021, Democrats controlled the House and—because Georgia's newly elected senators had not yet been seated on January 6—Republicans still controlled the Senate. That partisan split would not have mattered, though. As we saw in their votes on the objections to counting Arizona's and Pennsylvania's electoral votes, neither chamber would have gone along with a Pence power play.

But Eastman argued that Congress's votes in the Joint Session would not have mattered. On his theory of the vice president's power, whether Congress would have agreed with the vice president just wasn't relevant, because the Constitution gives the vice president unilateral and unreviewable power. On Eastman's theory, Congress would have no power to overrule his decision, just as Congress has no power to overrule the president's decision to issue a pardon. The Constitution, on Eastman's theory, gives the vice president the power to count votes; if Congress attempted to overrule his decisions, Congress would be acting unconstitutionally.

It's an astonishing theory. Yet Eastman didn't simply declare it as his own. Instead, he represented it as a mainstream theory among legal scholars, writing that "there is very solid legal authority, and historical precedent, for the view that the President of the Senate does the counting, including the resolution of disputed electoral votes (as Adams and Jefferson did while Vice President, regarding their own election as President), and all the Members of Congress can do is watch." Later in the same memo he concludes: "The fact is that the Constitution assigns this power to the Vice President as the ultimate arbiter."[5]

There is a lot packed into those sixty-nine words, and most of it is just flatly false. Let's take it step by step.

- "There is very solid legal authority, and historical precedent"

By "solid legal authority," lawyers typically mean either the plain text of the Constitution, a clear interpretation of the text by the Supreme Court, or an overwhelming consensus among scholars and academics agreeing on the position claimed. None of that is true for Eastman's claim. On the key question, the text is not clear. The vice president has the constitutional duty to "open" the certificates. But the use of the passive voice about the "counting" means that at the very least, it is not clear who has the constitutional authority over that critical task. No court has ever considered the matter; and there was at the time exactly *one* law review article in the history of the legal academy that seemingly agreed with the conclusion that Eastman asserted was settled.[6]

First, let's start with what can't be denied: never in the history of the Republic has any vice president discarded the certified electoral votes of any state over the express objection of any member of Congress. That's the precise pattern we're considering here. That simply had never happened before—and so, for that at least, there is indisputably no "historical precedent."

So what "historical precedent" was Eastman referring to? At best, it's extremely shaky. The source of that precedent is that one law review article suggesting something close to what Eastman claimed.[7]

That article was written by one of America's leading law professors, Yale professor Bruce Ackerman, and David Fontana, then a student at Yale and now a prominent law professor at George Washington University. The article was published in 2004. Its premise—the bit of history that made it interesting—was a discovery the authors had made about the "Certificate of Electoral Votes" submitted by Georgia in 1800. It turns out, Ackerman and Fontana claimed, that there were technical flaws in that certificate. The electors were meant to sign the document in a different place than they actually did, and the certificate was meant to list the electors differently than how it did.[8] Those flaws, *arguably*, in some hyper-strict technical universe, rendered the certificate invalid. If it was invalid, then Thomas Jefferson would not have won the presidency over John Adams in 1800.[9] Yet—and this was the sexy bit that made the article interesting—it was Jefferson himself who, as vice president, presided when the flaws in the certificate were overlooked. It's for this reason that Ackerman and Fontana had suggested in the title of their article that Jefferson "counted himself into the presidency."

If we look deeper, the story only gets more sordid. Something oddly similar had happened four years earlier, but with the roles reversed. In 1796, John Adams was the vice president and was running for president. Like Jefferson four years later, Adams presided over the count of electoral votes in which he himself was a candidate. Amazingly, in 1796 as in 1800, there was a question, or at least a rumor, about the validity of a state's purported electoral votes. In this case, the state was Vermont. The certificate Congress received named Adams's electors, but newspapers reported rumors that the votes were improper. As in 1800, the flaw was only a technicality. No one doubted that Adams, the arch-Federalist, had won the electors in the heart of Federalist Vermont. But partisan Jeffersonian newspapers alleged—without merit—that Vermont's legislature had violated the state's constitution and federal law in determining the manner for selecting the electors.[10]

If Adams "counted" the votes for himself, he would have won. If he didn't, he would have lost. Like Jefferson in 1800, Adams presided over a count that awarded Vermont's electoral votes to himself. But there was one critical difference: unlike Jefferson four years later, after Adams announced that Vermont's electors had voted for him, he sat down. That pause arguably gave members of Congress a chance to object to his ruling.

Jefferson didn't sit down in 1800—at least according to the best records we have. The tellers—the members of Congress appointed to tabulate the electoral votes—told Jefferson that Georgia's certificate looked amiss. But Jefferson didn't sit or pause to give Congress an obvious moment to object.

That difference has led some to wonder whether Jefferson's actions reflected the view that the vice president made a final decision about counting electoral votes, regardless of whether Congress disagreed. If it was final, the argument goes, then that would serve as historical precedent for what Eastman was urging Pence to do: to rule on the contested electoral votes without Congress having any chance to second-guess him.

But none of this follows from this thin reed of evidence.

First, even if Jefferson thought that his ruling was unreviewable—we don't think he did, but even if—Adams did not. The whole point about Adams sitting down between his announcing his decision about Vermont's votes and then declaring the result is that he obviously did view the matter as subject to objection. And if he did, then he didn't believe Eastman's theory that the vice president's power is unreviewable. Adams believed, at most, that the vice president has the power of any presiding officer: to make rulings, subject to reversal by the body he is presiding over. Even if Jefferson thought differently, that certainly wouldn't settle the constitutional question. Jefferson held fringe views about many aspects of the Constitution—which he played no part in drafting, because he was in France at the time. No doubt, Jefferson was a brilliant thinker; that doesn't make his thoughts constitutional law.

In any case, there is no evidence that Jefferson believed in Eastman's theory either. Nothing in the story about Jefferson presiding over the count of electoral votes in 1801 suggests that he thought that the vice president possessed an unreviewable power to determine which electoral votes to count. Why? Because in context, his ruling was so obviously correct, and no one—literally not one member of Congress—questioned it. *Maybe* Georgia's electors had violated technical rules about how the state's electoral votes were to be reported. But the question was whether a violation of form should suffice to disenfranchise Georgia's voters. No one suggested that Georgians actually preferred Adams over Jefferson. No one suggested that the certificates were substantively wrong. In the face of the voters' clear preference, no decent member of either party could have argued that Georgia's electoral votes should be discarded on purely technical grounds and thereby swing the presidency to someone else. To drive that point home, it turns out that Missouri's electoral votes for Trump in both 2016 and 2020 suffered from the same formal defect.[11] We very much doubt that Trump and his supporters would have approved if Vice President Biden rejected Missouri's electoral votes of 2016 on that basis.

And no one ever did argue that point, even though the tellers, the people who tabulated the electoral votes, included two Federalist members of Congress who were desperate to deny Jefferson the presidency. Even *they* didn't suggest that the Georgia electors' minor mistake in filling out the certificate—in only the second contested presidential election in American history—should disqualify the state's electoral votes.

Jefferson's subtle difference in posture—standing rather than sitting—hardly amounts to an exercise of the extraordinary power to "count himself into the presidency." No one had ever suggested that Georgia's electoral votes should be discarded. That Jefferson didn't explicitly pause for some member of Congress to enter an objection that no one had even mentioned therefore indicates nothing at all about what Jefferson thought his powers to be. To the contrary, his moving on was simply a recognition that there was no reason to pause. No one was questioning the results.

In an alternative version of history, we might have learned more about Jefferson's views of his powers. Imagine that scores of Federalists had made speeches demanding that Georgia's electoral votes be discarded. And imagine that Jefferson simply ignored them and proceeded to count Georgia's electoral votes over Congress's objections. Then imagine that many people, in Congress and elsewhere, criticized Jefferson for counting those votes but didn't question his power to do so. In that version of history, the episode might support the idea that the vice president had a constitutional authority to count the votes, whatever Congress says or objects to notwithstanding. But none of that happened. The real history we have tells us nothing about any special constitutional power for the vice president.

The two authors of the one law review article Eastman relied upon ultimately agree with our conclusion. In the podcast we hosted leading up to the election, we invited David Fontana to comment on his piece. He rejected the idea completely: "All observers from both major political parties at the time . . . thought that it was not just for Adams and Jefferson to decide [which electoral votes should be counted]. Adams made that very clear by sitting down. . . . Jefferson after the fact would say to people—and this was reported in all sorts of newspapers—that he thought it meaningful that the Federalists did not object."[12]

And in his later writing reflecting on this period, Bruce Ackerman explains Jefferson's actions as an exercise in conciliatory statecraft, to avoid an open conflict so early in the Republic, rather than an exercise of raw constitutional power. Neither author believes that the evidence supports the conclusion that the vice president has a constitutional power to determine which electoral votes will count. Yet that didn't stop John Eastman from relying upon their article to justify the vice president overturning the election in 2020.

The next claim in Eastman's memo is that

- "the President of the Senate does the counting, including the resolution of disputed electoral votes (as Adams and Jefferson did while Vice President, regarding their own election as President)."

Here the historical evidence is overwhelming: the "President of the Senate" does *not* do "the counting." In every election since 1792, Congress did the counting through the tellers they appointed. The vice president, in each of those elections, reported the counts the tellers had given him. In no election did the vice president purport to count electors differently from how the tellers did.

That is even true in the case of allegedly "disputed electoral votes." Again, the votes in 1796 and 1800 were not "disputed," certainly not on the floor of the Joint Session. Yes, Jefferson and Adams announced the result that the votes counted; but there's no evidence that they did so against the views of anyone, and the tellers were the ones who did the actual counting.

Back to Eastman's memo:

• "and all the Members of Congress can do is watch."

There is no evidence from the text of the Constitution or from the historical record that all the "Members of Congress" *can* do is watch. To establish that claim, we would have to have one or more cases where a member tried to object and his (and at the founding, it was only "his") objection was overruled or ignored. But there are literally no cases in which an objection is raised and ignored. Adams's behavior suggests that an objection would have been entertained, had anyone cared to make one. No one did.

Putting this all together, we're going to do something that is rare in the law—we're going to make a claim without any qualifications attached to it: it is plainly wrong to suggest that the vice president has any independent constitutional authority to count electoral votes or determine their validity against the will of Congress. She may have the power to make a preliminary announcement from the chair on which votes shall be counted, based on what the tellers have reported to her. And that ruling can set a default that can be overcome only with the right kind of majority vote. (We'll see the consequence of this in chapter 5.) But nothing in the text of the Constitution, in any legal authority interpreting that text, or in any historical precedent suggests that the vice president has any powers here that might trump the power of Congress.

We can be thankful that in 2021, Pence relied on sound constitutional analysis rather than Eastman's wild theory. In the days leading up to January 6, a respected and conservative former federal judge, J. Michael Luttig, who was a former clerk to Justice Antonin Scalia and long considered a frontrunner for a Republican Supreme Court appointment, advised Vice President Pence that "Professor Eastman was incorrect at every turn of the analysis in his January 2 memorandum."[13] As rioters stormed the Capitol, Pence's chief counsel, Greg Jacob, sent Eastman an email telling him that it was "gravely, gravely irresponsible for you to entice the President with an academic theory that had no legal viability, and that you well know would lose before any judge who heard and decided the case."[14] These conservatives were right. Eastman was wrong.

What this means—with certainty—is that no vice president has the unilateral power to determine which electoral votes count. Any preliminary ruling the vice president might make is subject to reversal by the Joint Session of Congress. The vice president acts as a presiding officer with respect to a vote-counting process that is directly controlled by Congress. Thus no one, including Donald Trump in 2021, Joe Biden in 2025, or any other future president, can count on their vice president to rule them into office.

There is one further puzzle from the 2020 election, however, that it is worth flagging now. What about the alternative slates of electors?

On Election Day, in every state, there are at least two slates of presidential electors, one assigned to each candidate. In all but two states, the winner of the popular vote in that state determines which slate of electors is appointed for that state. The other slates that didn't win—the "alternative" slates—almost always drop out of the process after that. But though they lurk in the background, the case of Hawaii in 1960 shows their critical potential.

In 1960, though unofficial tallies reported Hawaii's popular vote had gone for Senator John F. Kennedy, the state's first presidential vote was initially declared for Vice President Richard M. Nixon. The Republican electors were accordingly declared the winners, at least at first. The lieutenant governor of Hawaii, a Republican and at the time the acting governor (because the governor was out of the state), certified Nixon's slate of electors at the end of November.

The popular vote was exceptionally close. And suspiciously, the initial tallies showed mathematical inconsistencies. A lawyer for the Hawaii Democratic Party, Robert Dodge, asked for a recount under state law. That recount, completed on December 28, determined that Kennedy had won the state after all. The governor dutifully sent Congress a second certificate, this time indicating that it should count Kennedy's electors. Because that determination was made just days before Congress was to vote, the post office had to make special efforts to assure that the certificates arrived in time.

The catch was this: the Constitution does not speak of counting electors; it speaks of counting electoral votes. The dispute in Hawaii was, of course, about which slate of electors had won the popular election and thus which slate should have been appointed. But that wasn't the only question. The next question was whether the electors had cast their electoral votes—and, critically for constitutional purposes, when. The Constitution directs that the vote of electors in the Electoral College must happen on the same day. (In 1856, a snowstorm stopped Wisconsin electors from voting on the right day. Congress spent two days debating whether that delay disqualified their votes. It ultimately punted on the question because James Buchanan won the election with or without Wisconsin's electoral votes.) What happens if, as in Hawaii, the identity of the legally recognized, validly appointed electors shifts after the electors cast their vote in the Electoral College?

The lawyer representing the Democratic Party in Hawaii saw the problem.[15] And so, even though those electors were not, according to the legal process as it had played out to that point, actually the electors thought chosen by the voters of Hawaii *at the time they voted*, those Kennedy electors gathered together on the legally appointed day and cast their votes for John Kennedy. When the courts finally resolved that Kennedy had indeed won the state, there were votes cast by Kennedy electors on the right day for Congress to count.

Jump ahead sixty years: Hawaii's story may not be well known to the public, but it was not lost to history. When the Trump campaign realized that its fight was going to extend beyond December 14, the day when the electors would vote, it had its slates follow Hawaii's example. In seven states that had certified Joe Biden as the winner, the Trump electors met on December 14 and cast their votes for Donald Trump; those Trump electors' votes were then sent to the archivist of the United States.[16] The "certificates" bearing those votes were available to the vice president as Congress convened on January 6.

Here, however, is the puzzle: the Electoral Count Act (ECA)—the statute that governs how presidents get elected, and a statute we'll examine in detail in chapter 5—requires that the vice president lay before the Joint Session "all the certificates *and papers purporting to be certificates* of the electoral votes" (emphasis added). These alternative certificates were certainly certificates "purporting to be certificates of the electoral vote"—at least in the sense that the pieces of paper themselves *claimed* to be the legitimate certificates of the legitimate electoral votes. Yet strikingly, Mike Pence did not include them in the declaration that he made on January 6. As he reported it, there was only one slate of electors from every state (and the District of Columbia). But we know that there were at least two from seven states that "purport[ed] to be" certificates.

That Pence recognized the difference showed in his introductory statement about the electoral votes from each state. On prior January 6s, the vice president opened the Joint Session with standard language: "After ascertainment has been had that the certificates are authentic and correct in form, the tellers will count and make a list of the votes of the electors of the several States." But on January 6, 2021, Pence added something critical: "After ascertainment has been had that the certificates are authentic and correct in form, the tellers will count and make a list of the votes of the electors of each State, beginning with Alabama, *which the parliamentarian has advised me is the only certificate of vote from that state that purports to be a return from that state that has annexed to it a certificate from an authority of that state purporting to appoint or ascertain electors.*"

That extra language did not come from the Constitution or the Electoral Count Act. Why did Pence add it? The reason is a ruling by the parliamentarian that made sense in 2020 but may cause real trouble going forward. According to the parliamentarian, section 15 ("Counting electoral votes in Congress") of the ECA must be read alongside section 6 ("Credentials of electors"). And according to section 6, it is the governor ("the executive") of each state who has a "duty" to "communicate by registered mail under the seal of the State to the Archivist of the United States a certificate of such ascertainment of the electors appointed." The parliamentarian's view was that, read together, these two sections meant that the only certificates the vice president had to present to the Joint Session were those that went with electors who had a "certificate" from the governor that "ascertain[ed]" that they were "the electors appointed" as specified in section 6. Thus, even if the certificates of the votes from the alternative slates of electors arrived in Washington, they wouldn't be considered because they didn't come with a certificate from a state official purporting to appoint them as electors.

That was the right call in 2020. None of the alternative slates had any legal basis for being counted by the Joint Session. Some were literally fraudulent.[17] Though the electors had voted when they needed to vote and had signed the appropriate certificates, no legal authority ever upheld their claim to represent their state. There was no reason to waste Congress's time with those certificates.

But as we'll see in chapter 5, this reading of the Electoral Count Act's rules could cause significant problems in the future. And the complications only compound under the new Electoral Count Reform Act. To put it in a form that is too compact now but that we'll explain more below: if the governor goes rogue and certifies the wrong slate of electors, then under the parliamentarian's understanding, the right slate has no obvious path to the floor of the Joint Session. That's not *certain* to flip the results from the democratically correct outcome. But it certainly could.

---

tl;dr

The strategy: The vice president exercises an exclusive constitutional power to count the votes as he or she thinks proper.

The chance that this strategy flips the results in 2025: none

The chance that this strategy flips results in future elections: none

Summary why: An election cannot be reversed by the unilateral action of the vice president. This path is a clear loser for any takeover, whether Red or Blue.

But: We are certain that the vice president lacks the constitutional authority to determine which electors are valid. It's worth asking, however, what the world would have looked like if a vice president tried anyway. Imagine that Vice President Pence, instead of abiding by his constitutional and moral duties, had listened to the mob and announced that he was rejecting the Biden electors from seven states, and that without those electoral votes Pence and President Trump had won reelection.

---

continued

That would have precipitated perhaps the most serious constitutional crisis in our history, rivaled only by the Civil War. There is no doubt that Democrats—along with, one hopes, many law-abiding Republicans—would have sprinted to the courts seeking a judicial order that Pence's move was unconstitutional and legally void. And one hopes the courts would have given it to them.

And yet two lingering risks haunt us. The first is that, because of the political question doctrine—the principle that courts don't get involved in resolving issues that the Constitution commits to one of the political branches—the courts might have refused to rule on the case. If that happened, we would have faced a standoff between Congress and the president with no historical precedent and no obvious and peaceful way to resolve. The second, and even more chilling, possibility is if the courts *did* rule in favor of Congress but, citing a crackpot legal theory that the courts rejected, the president and vice president refused to vacate the White House anyway.

There is absolutely no doubt that as a matter of constitutional law, the vice president doesn't have this extravagant power to declare the next president. But we should also retain a sober perspective on the limitations on the practical power of law—even wise and just law—to ensure the right outcomes. Or, in this case, to ensure the mere continuation of the United States as a functioning constitutional democracy. As we will see throughout the remainder of this book, the law must ultimately rely on the good faith of the people who hold power. In the absence of good faith, that dependence creates catastrophic risks.

4

"Faithless" Electors

On November 8, 2016, Donald Trump received 62,984,828 votes for president. Hillary Clinton received 2,868,686 more—65,853,514. Clinton thus beat Trump by 2.1 points. And yet because of the way Trump's votes were distributed across the states, he appeared on track to receive 74 more electoral votes than she did. In the end, Trump received 77 more electoral voters than Clinton. The loser of the national popular vote had thus won the election.

In 2012, when Donald Trump believed that the same thing had happened, but favoring the Democrats, he called for a "revolution." Early forecasts had predicted that Mitt Romney would win the popular vote but that Barack Obama would win in the Electoral College. Trump was outraged. ("The electoral college is a disaster for a democracy.")[1] But by 2016, Trump's views on the Electoral College had evolved. ("I was never a fan of the Electoral College until now.")[2] Though he hadn't won a plurality of the popular vote, he had won the vote in 60 percent of the states.

Shortly after the election, two Clinton electors in two different states began to think about how to respond. Yes, George W. Bush had been elected president in 2000 despite losing the popular vote, but his margin of loss was tiny—half a percentage point. Trump's loss was four times that. That difference led these two electors—and millions of Americans across the country—to begin to wonder whether the

United States was really committed to inaugurating a man who had lost the popular vote so badly.

That question shifted the public's attention to the institution that stood between the popular vote and inauguration: the Electoral College. Created by the Framers as a way to select a president who would not be dependent on either Congress or state legislatures, the college was to be populated by "electors." Those "electors" were people. The Framers of the Constitution anticipated that the electors would be pillars of the community who could be trusted to make a wise selection of a statesman for president. The presumption was that electors would have a choice about whom to vote for and would exercise real discretion in casting their votes.

To see the point, consider the only other place in the original Constitution where the word "elector" is used. Article I, establishing Congress, sets out the procedure for electing the House of Representatives. As the text puts it, "The House of Representatives shall be composed of Members chosen every second Year by the People of the several States, and the Electors in each State shall have the Qualifications requisite for Electors of the most numerous Branch of the State Legislature." Those "electors" are what we call "voters." This clause specifies that the people eligible to vote for members of the House shall be the same as those eligible to select "the most numerous Branch of the State Legislature." In other words, if state law authorizes you to vote for representatives to the most numerous branch of your state legislature, then the Constitution authorizes you to vote for Congress.

Yet no one would imagine those "electors"—aka "voters"—could be directed by state law to vote one way or another. No one would think, for example, that Democratic Massachusetts could make it a misdemeanor to vote for a Republican. The very idea of a "voter" in a free society is someone who has, as the Framers put it, a "right of choice." So, too, with an "elector," whether of Congress or of the president.

Contrary to that commonsense democratic notion of a voter's freedom, however, dozens of states have passed laws that bind presidential electors to vote in the Electoral College for the candidate that won the popular vote in that state. That's why, even though you're technically voting for an elector when you vote in a presidential election, the elector's name appears only in fine print below the candidate's— if it appears at all. When you pull the lever for a candidate, you're really voting for an elector who is "pledged" to vote for the candidate named on the ballot. In some states, that pledge is made legally binding.

Are such laws constitutional?

They certainly don't fit with the Framers' vision of "electors." After the election in 2016, one of us (Lessig) wrote an op-ed in the *Washington Post* arguing that every presidential elector should recognize the moral force of the popular vote and that they were free to cast their ballots for the winner of the popular vote, any pledge or state law notwithstanding.

Many called that essay constitutionally wrong and politically naive. It certainly was politically naive. There was no way any committed Trump elector was going to vote for Hillary Clinton. At least, they would not do it without first experiencing the political equivalent of a religious conversion and then entering a witness protection program for electors.

The two electors we mentioned at the beginning of this chapter were not as naive as Lessig. They knew that no Republican electors would cast a vote for a Democrat. But each, independently, began to wonder whether he couldn't convince enough Republican electors to vote for a Republican other than Donald Trump. Under the count as it seemed it would be at the time, if thirty-seven did that, Trump would be denied a majority in the Electoral College, and the House of Representatives would then be required to choose among the top three electoral college vote-getters.[3] Because each state receives one vote in the House, and there were thirty-two states with Republican-majority delegations after the election in 2016, it was clear that the House would eventually elect a Republican.[4] But that Republican might well not have been Donald Trump.

These two electors—Bret Chiafalo and Micheal Baca—discovered each other on social media. They quickly began working together to try to rally enough electors to this third-way election. They knew they needed to make it credible that they were not simply trying to elect Hillary Clinton. So their first task was to recruit thirty-seven Democratic electors to join them and to pledge to cast their vote not for Hillary Clinton, but for a Republican. Once they had those Democratic electors, they would try to recruit thirty-seven Republican electors to match.

The electors formed a group they called the Hamilton Electors. They were inspired to that name by the way Alexander Hamilton described the Electoral College in the Federalist Papers: "A small number of persons, selected by their fellow-citizens from the general mass, will be most likely to possess the information and discernment requisite to such complicated investigations. . . . And as the electors, chosen in each State, are to assemble and vote in the State in which they are chosen, this detached and divided situation will expose them much less to heats and ferments, which might be communicated from them to the people, than if they were all to be convened at one time, in one place."[5]

That's precisely the role these electors wanted to play in 2016, and they organized as hard as they could to help bring that vision to life.

Lessig had nothing to do with this organizing. But because he believed that these electors indeed did have the right to cast their votes in whatever manner they believed proper, he helped organize a legal structure—the Electors' Trust—to support them in their work. The trust would defend independent electors against legal (or other, more frightening) threats and help coordinate their efforts, if they indeed decided to vote their conscience rather than vote as they were pledged. The Electors' Trust hired lawyers who gave legal advice to these electors, without revealing to Lessig or anyone behind the trust the identities of the people they were advising. Even though Lessig had started the fund, he had no idea how many were seeking the lawyers' advice or what the electors planned to do.

But he did have a sense of what was brewing, from conversations with a prominent Republican who was quietly speaking with Republican electors about the threat he and others thought Donald Trump posed. This Republican, R. J. Lyman, estimated between 20 and 40 Republican electors were actively considering a vote against Donald Trump. Lessig had no way to verify these numbers. But subsequent survey research done by one of the most careful students of actual presidential electors, Robert Alexander, was consistent with Lyman's estimate. According to Alexander, 20 percent of Republican electors "gave some thought to defecting."[6] Twenty percent of 306 is 61 electors—more than enough to deprive Trump of an Electoral College majority.

Every one of those electors knew that they could face grave consequences if they voted their conscience and against Donald Trump. Each was considering carefully whether to accept those consequences. All but two determined that they would not jump unless their vote would make a difference. The Electors' Trust was designed to address this concern by providing assurances to those electors about the total who were willing to vote contrary to their pledge. If that number approached the number needed to flip the results, then the Electors' Trust would assure the electors that enough had committed to the plan. If that assurance was sufficient, and if the electors held firm, their votes on December 19, 2016, would have sent the election to the House of Representatives.

In the weeks between the election and the day the electors voted, Chiafalo and Baca worked feverishly with a team of volunteers to recruit electors to their cause. You know how this story ends, so you can work out what happened. Though they were buoyed by hope during their monthlong campaign—especially after Christopher Suprun, a Republican elector from Texas, publicly announced in a *New York Times* op-ed that he would not vote for Trump—in the end, they could not promise the Republican electors that they could deliver enough votes against Trump to make a difference. On December 19, 2 Republican electors and 8 Democratic electors tried to vote contrary to their pledge. The Republican votes were recorded (which is why Trump received only 304 electoral votes rather than the 306 pledged to him); 3 of the 8 Democratic electors were replaced by state officials with other electors, leaving the votes of just 5 as part of the official record.

What the Hamilton Electors tried to do made sense from the perspective of the Framers. The Framers did not establish a direct method for electing a president. Such a system would have been wholly impractical in 1787. It took four months for news to move from one corner of the nation to the other. How could a candidate ever hope to campaign to the whole nation? Many of the Framers at the Constitutional Convention also feared what Elbridge Gerry of Massachusetts called "an excess of democracy"—because, Gerry said, "the people do not want virtue, but are the dupes of pretended patriots."[7] Instead, the Framers created a temporary body that would be called into existence every four years to select a president. That body, or as it has come to be known, "college," would be populated by "electors" who would be chosen through a process determined by state legislatures. But in the Framers' vision, those electors would ultimately exercise their own judgment about who should be president.

That judgment would not be unconstrained. Nobody imagined the electors as philosopher-kings. Nobody thought they were turning over to the electors the power to choose just anyone, from anywhere, as the next president. To the contrary, state legislatures were very keen to determine who the electors would vote for, because from the first contested presidential election in 1796, legislatures tried to align themselves with emerging political power.

At first, state legislatures tried to exercise that influence by choosing the electors themselves. Between 1796 and 1832, legislatures cycled through many procedures for choosing electors. In 1800, for example, ten states had their electors chosen directly by the legislature, two through a statewide general election, three through elections in districts, and one by a combination of methods. But as the state legislatures changed the election process, the naked partisanship of the system began to disgust Americans.[8] By the mid-1830s, politicians were promising to bind themselves to a political mast by turning over the choice of presidential electors to their states' voters. After 1836, the only states where legislatures chose their electors directly were those just transitioning from being a territory to a state, such as Colorado in 1876, or emerging from Reconstruction, such as Florida in 1868. The sole exception was South Carolina, where the legislature appointed electors through the election of 1860.

Yet even though the legislatures had clear preferences, they always understood that they couldn't control their electors directly. There was always the chance that something would inspire an elector, no matter how carefully vetted, to cast their vote in a way contrary to how they were expected to vote. But throughout American history, it almost never happened. In the history of the Electoral College, before 2016 there was exactly one time (among 23,507 votes cast since

1789) that an elector flipped their vote and voted for the principal opponent of the candidate they were pledged to support. This was the first and most famous "faithless elector": Samuel Miles, who was meant to support Adams in 1796 but who voted for Jefferson instead.[9]

The Hamilton Electors should have taken Sam Miles's name, not Hamilton's, since Miles, too, was motivated by a desire to assure a result more closely matching the will of "the People." Like Miles, the Hamilton Electors understood that they had been appointed to vote for their party's nominated candidate; and like Miles, they found it morally significant that the public had voted to the contrary. Reflecting a plausibly dominant modern view about the relevance of the popular vote, the Hamilton Electors were acting on the belief that who won the national popular vote should matter, even if it couldn't matter directly. They wanted to adjust their vote to produce a result closer to the national popular vote, even if not mirroring it. No, Clinton would not be president. But it should be Congress that decided whether the man she beat should be president in her stead.

Had they succeeded, no one knows what would have happened. Some said it would have provoked a civil war. Lessig didn't think so in 2016. After January 6, he is not as sure. Everything would have depended on how the House responded. It could have chosen Trump, it could have chosen Clinton, or it could have chosen the compromise Republican candidate, who no doubt would have pledged a period of healing.

If the House had taken the third option, and if peace had in fact prevailed, then this method for dealing with inverted elections might well have become a norm. In response, states might have felt that they needed some way to constrain the actions of electors. But when the electors are simply advancing democratic ends—as the Hamilton Electors plainly were—there would be no good (nonpartisan) reason to block them and no constitutional reason to give states the powers to block them. If the Electoral College, in other words, became a safety valve on the process for electing the president to preserve democratically legitimate results, then it could function to avoid election misfires and presidencies constantly challenged by questions about their legitimacy.

If the House played that function, it would also reduce the incentive for presidential campaigns to focus on crafting Electoral College victories rather than popular majorities. Of course, a candidate would always want both. But candidates would know that their chances of being elected would be harmed if they did not prevail in both. That would change presidential campaigns. And that change would only improve the democratic process that elects our president. The freedom the Framers meant the electors to have could thus have helped the Electoral College navigate inverted elections while improving democratic responsiveness generally.

Yet that benefit would be purchased with a significant risk. If electors are legally free—either absolutely, because the state has no power to control them, or relatively, because the state could control them only if they were acting against a democratic ideal—there would always be a risk that electors, for good or bad reasons, could be influenced to vote contrary to their pledge. Recognizing elector freedom, in other words, would not come without potential costs.

It was that potential cost that was clearly on the minds of the Supreme Court justices when they finally had a chance to review the issue. Of the eight Democrats who joined the Hamilton Electors, one was removed as an elector before his vote was counted: Micheal Baca of Colorado. Four others were fined one thousand dollars for their vote: Bret Chiafalo, Levi Guerra, Esther John, and Robert Satiacum Jr. of Washington State. Baca and three of the Washington electors challenged the actions of the states, and in May 2020 their challenge ended up before the United States Supreme Court. Lessig argued the case for the Washington electors—from his desk at Harvard, since the Court was holding arguments by telephone during the pandemic. Jason Harrow argued for Micheal Baca. Two months later, the Court rejected the electors' arguments and upheld the power of states to control how electors may vote.

From the perspective of history and the original meaning of the Constitution, the decision of the Court was plainly wrong. One of America's leading originalists, Michael Rappaport, called it an "originalist disaster."[10] And as we'll see in chapter 9, the decision turns out to open up the most likely path for a stolen election.

Yet in the middle of a pandemic, leading into a terrifying presidential election, with—let's just be open about it—Donald Trump as a candidate, the Supreme Court was not focused on original meaning alone. It was also focused on the threat of corruption. Question after question during the oral argument asked about the risk of an elector being bribed to cast their vote for the candidate opposing the one to whom they were pledged. Regardless of fidelity to the Constitution's original meaning, the Supreme Court was not about to increase the anxiety around the election of 2020 by amplifying the risk of electors going rogue.

At the time of the decision, this concern about bribery seemed absurd. In the history of the 23,507 electoral votes cast since the founding, never once has there been a suggestion of bribery. One amicus brief made the flatly false argument that the bribery of electors would not be punishable under existing federal law, which it certainly would be. That fact would prevent the most egregious instances of corruption: if, in a close election, a Republican elector mysteriously votes for the Democrat in a context where there is no public-regarding reason for the flipped vote (such as an inverted election or a credible claim of incapacity), you can be certain that prosecutors would look carefully at that elector's finances. And it would certainly be very hard for a corrupt elector to hide any significant bribe from those prosecutors. ("I found the million dollars on the side of the road! Honestly, I did!!")

After January 6, however, it may make sense to worry about influences that might flip an elector's vote. Many state election officials were extraordinarily brave in 2020, standing up to the false claims of fraud raised by President Trump's campaign. But if the Court had held that electors were free, how many would have been "persuaded" to vote against their pledges, not through bribes but through fear? Now that violence against the members of Congress counting electoral votes is a historical fact, it is not hard to imagine effective threats of retribution against electors themselves.

Regardless, the matter was decided. Justice Elena Kagan wrote for eight justices, and Justice Thomas concurred. Electors had no constitutional right to vote their conscience—even if their conscience was consistent with the will of the voters. "Here," Kagan concluded, grabbing for dramatic significance, "We the People rule."[11]

The relevance of all this to the argument of this book is direct and indirect. We'll end this chapter with the direct and return to the indirect in chapter 9.

It has long been feared that an election could be stolen by, as Rick Hasen put it, "a handful of faithless electors."[12] As relates to the argument of this book, one might well worry that an election might be stolen by faithless electors being induced to vote, contrary to their pledge, for the candidate on the other side. With the decision in *The Electors Cases* (both *Chiafalo v. Washington* and *Colorado Department of State v. Baca*), the Supreme Court has enabled states to remove this risk. The consequence is that states are now free to regulate how electors vote—and free to remove electors who vote contrary to their pledge.

Chiafalo, however, is only the first step to removing the risk that faithless electors pose to presidential elections. If it acted on the power the Court has now affirmed, a state could eliminate any elector risk by adopting a statute that automatically removes an elector who tries to vote contrary to their pledge. As we'll explain below, those statutes must deal with a critical problem created by the Twentieth Amendment. But if the states pass laws binding electors that address this constitutional problem, faithless electors will not be a risk in the next presidential election.

But if the states don't take this step, then a critical risk remains. *Chiafalo* only affirms the state's power to regulate how electors vote— or, if it chooses, not to regulate their votes. The case does not hold that the Constitution requires that electors must always vote as expected. It simply allows the states to direct a vote and to attach consequences to the decision to vote contrary to the law. Those consequences could be a fine (as it was for the Washington State electors) or the removal of the elector (as it was for Micheal Baca in Colorado). Or a state might continue to permit its electors to violate their pledges without any consequence at all.

But if the state permits the faithless vote to be *cast,* even if the elector is later fined or even imprisoned, the vote still counts. That fact—in the current political context—creates a great risk. By permitting a faithless elector's vote to be cast and counted, a state puts a bull's-eye on the electors' backs and creates the risk of intense pressure campaigns and even threats of violence.

Imagine again the scenario we've described. A MAGA Republican wins the popular vote by a slight margin; Joe Biden wins in the Electoral College. North Carolina has voted for Biden, but if the electors in North Carolina vote for the MAGA Republican, the Republican will have won both the popular and the electoral college votes.

The state legislature repeals its law binding electors to vote as they were pledged.[13]

Next imagine that the MAGA Republican candidate and their campaign start raising a storm of fury about presidential electors and the popular vote. North Carolina law had regulated how the electors voted; assume that the legislature repeals that law. Next, the campaign begins to argue that the electors in North Carolina—even though pledged to Biden—should, like Samuel Miles in 1796, vote for the candidate "who actually won." Imagine that supporters of the campaign begin to pressure the electors. In 2016, many electors were threatened before they cast their votes. After January 6, those threats could well seem more significant and bear the terrifying aura of plausibility.

How many electors would resist the threats and vote for the candidate to whom they were pledged? How many would heed the former president's call to "do the right thing" and flip to the other side—knowing that in the last election, his call for Vice President Pence to "do the right thing" was followed mere minutes later by a mob chanting "Hang Mike Pence" at the base of a gallows erected on the Capitol steps after Pence refused? How much faith, in other words, should we place in these anonymous, unpaid public officials to do the right thing regardless of the consequence to them? (As we'll see below, Congress could conceivably reject the vote of a coerced elector [as a vote not "regularly given"], but that would require the agreement of both houses of Congress and would still not restore the vote to how it should have been originally given.)

Don't get us wrong. Presidential electors are by far the least corrupted branch of our federal constitutional system. There is not a single example in the history of the Republic of an elector being bribed to switch sides (the same cannot be said of Congress or the president); nor is there any example of an elector being coerced to flip their vote.

The only elector who flipped sides—Samuel Miles—did so for purely democratic reasons. The trust the Framers placed in electors has been validated by a history of honorable service.

But as the norms of our constitutional republic collapse, the threats become different. And unless states act immediately to close the gap left open by *Chiafalo*, faithless electors remain an important risk. In chapter 10, we explain how states should address that risk. Until they do, this risk remains especially prominent.

---

tl;dr

The strategy: To coerce the electors not required by state law to vote for the pledged candidate to flip their votes to support the MAGA Republican.

The chance that this strategy flips the results in 2025: significant

The chance that this strategy flips results in future elections: significant

Summary why: The Supreme Court held that states could compel electors to vote for the candidate to whom they were pledged. But not all states have done so, and some of the states that already have such laws merely impose fines on faithless electors but don't automatically replace them. This leaves open the possibility that electors in those states could flip their votes. In normal times, that's not a risk. In the context of the threats of violence today, the risk is significant.

5

Rogue Governors

One century after we declared our independence from Britain, our democracy almost collapsed. Of course, the nation had, in an important sense, already collapsed fifteen years before. A civil war is not a badge of political health. But even during the Civil War, the institutions of the American presidential democracy continued to function. President Abraham Lincoln stood for reelection in a race that (by the standards of the time) was bitterly contested but more or less free and fair. The Union accepted the outcome.

But in 1876, the machine for selecting the president and vice president almost went off the rails. The election was extremely close. A fight over competing slates of electors in four states—Florida, Louisiana, Oregon, and South Carolina—left the ultimate result in doubt. There were disputes about which candidate had won in those states and thus questions about which slates of electors the state had appointed.[1] The opposing sides took an extraordinary step: the slate of electors from *both* candidates was sent to Congress to be counted.

Congress thus had to decide which of those competing slates to recognize. But Congress, too, was divided. As in 2020, Republicans held the Senate and Democrats held the House. Had one party controlled both chambers, the unified Congress could have recognized that party's slates of electors. That might have been a blatantly partisan way to resolve the dispute, but it would also have been definitive.

A divided Congress left no apparent way to break the impasse—and no way was specified in the Constitution.

Facing a mounting crisis, Congress appointed a special commission to decide which of the competing slates should be counted. Five Republicans, five Democrats, and five Supreme Court justices (only one of whom was thought to be remotely nonpartisan) were named to the commission, which ultimately recommended, by a single vote, that the Republican slates of electors be counted. Rutherford B. Hayes was thus granted a one-vote victory in the Electoral College—even though his opponent, Samuel Tilden, had won the popular vote by more than three points. It was the largest Electoral College inversion in the history of the Republic.

Students of history tend to forgive this inversion. Yes, they acknowledge, Tilden won the popular vote. But there was widespread fraud and violent suppression of African American voters throughout the nation, and in the South especially. That suppression, which deprived Hayes of countless votes, made Tilden's official three-point margin more a mirage than a mandate. A sense of rough justice leads most to believe that ultimate justice was done.

The suppression of African American votes was, without doubt, pervasive and violent. Had the election of 1876 been as protected as the election of 1872, when federal troops throughout the South defended polling places and the freedom to vote, who knows what the results would have been.

Strikingly, however, the swing vote on the commission ignored the claims of fraud and voter suppression. Joseph P. Bradley, one of the five Supreme Court justices on the commission, cast the deciding vote and issued lengthy opinions justifying his decision. He had rejected the Democrats' allegations of fraud—not as false but as irrelevant to the issue he was to decide. In each state, he affirmed the slate of electors certified by state authorities; in each state, he ignored the slate offered by those claiming fraud in the election.[2] Federalism required that he follow the rule of the states and not those seeking to besmirch the democratic process within those states.

The commission's decision came only shortly before Inauguration Day. Rumors of competing inauguration ceremonies and of militias preparing to march toward Washington swirled. Some in Congress refused to accept the commission's result until just days before Hayes was to take office. The conflict finally resolved when Democrats acquiesced to Hayes's election, allegedly based on a backroom deal to withdraw federal troops from the South, marking an end to Reconstruction. However morally compromised the bargain, militias had not burned the Capitol, so in the eyes of many, the bargain had averted a crisis. African Americans, who would suffer another near century of Jim Crow in the wake of the alleged deal, were understandably less convinced.

In the aftermath of the crisis, the politicians committed themselves to reforming the process for counting electoral votes. Yet it took over a decade for Congress to enact reforms intended to avoid a repeat of 1876. When they did, their work was cumbersome and convoluted. And though it has never misfired in a way that affected the results, the Electoral Count Act (ECA) presented a catastrophic risk in 2020 that—through a combination of the ineptness of Trump's legal maneuvering and the good faith of a few Republican governors—we were exceptionally lucky to avoid.

Thankfully, however, the ECA will not govern the election in 2024. As we were writing this book, Congress enacted the Electoral Count Reform Act of 2022 (ECRA). One of us (Seligman) had spent much of his time since the last election helping to craft that legislation, which fixes many of the most obvious flaws in the ECA. The law is a historic accomplishment, all the more astonishing because it required significant bipartisan cooperation to overcome a filibuster in the Senate.

No doubt, the ECRA makes it much more difficult to exploit the process through which states transmit their electoral votes to Congress. But as we will argue, under the critical assumption of the hypothetical driving the argument in this book—that the election in 2024 is close—it does not foreclose exploitation. Significant ambiguities remain in the law governing the election of the president. Those ambiguities could be used to flip the result—still.

To put this risk in context, we will first explain how the ECA could have been exploited in 2020. Then we'll describe how the ECRA could still be exploited in 2024 and beyond.

But we emphasize, before we map these possibilities, that the risks we're describing are risks only if conditions make the truth difficult to see. If there was one clearly hopeful sign from 2020, it was the integrity of the people who wished for different results but who would not bend the truth, or the law, to produce the results they wanted. That integrity depends upon it being clear that one side has won and the other has not. The experience of 2020 gives us hope the scenarios in this chapter will not come to pass, at least when the right answer is clear.

The behavior of three Republicans in 2020 makes this point for us. The type we fear the most is the kind evinced by Senator Josh Hawley (R-MO). As we'll explain in this chapter, Hawley's behavior was the most terrifyingly lawless. It was terrifying because he certainly knew better. It was lawless because the Electoral Count Act—and the Constitution—meant that his objections were literally without basis in the law. Yet a will to power bent him away from the truth and the law and helped rally to violence on January 6 the many who knew much less.

Senator Rand Paul (R-KY) is a hopeful contrast. Though he plainly believed that there were problems in the election of 2020 in the states—problems that undermined, in his view, the confidence that people had had in the election—he thought it plainly wrong for Congress to overturn the results as reported by the states. Sheltered during the violence that erupted on January 6, Paul tweeted, "I was planning to say I fear the chaos of establishing a precedent that Congress can overturn elections. Boy, was I right. Chaos. Anarchy. It's wrong and un-American."[3] As we will see below, that statement was consistent with what he had said before January 6: that Congress had no power to reverse the decisions in the states, even if Congress believed the states were mistaken in their decisions.

But the most hopeful example of all the Republicans was Senate Majority Leader Mitch McConnell (R-KY). McConnell is a vigorous partisan. We both have criticized his willingness to bend the rules or precedents to assure Republican victories. That willingness secured a conservative majority on the Supreme Court for a generation.

We have no way of knowing what McConnell considered as he led his caucus into the Joint Session on January 6. About allegations of fraud, he had said that Congress should wait and see. That led many to fear that he might be strategizing with the vice president to assure a Trump victory, regardless of the true results.

But on the morning of January 6, before any violence had broken out on the Capitol steps, McConnell gave a speech in the Senate that made clear his loyalty—to the institution of free elections and the integrity of their results, regardless whether that outcome favored Republicans or Democrats.[4] McConnell showed us that a partisan can sometimes transcend politics, that when there was a truth that honest souls could not deny, that truth would constrain to assure that crazy does not prevail.

In this chapter, we consider this hypothetical: a governor going "rogue" by acting contrary to what the votes of the people in that state demand. If that happens before January 6, 2025, we have no doubt there will be Josh Hawley–types, regardless. And we are certain there will be Rand Paul–types, too. But whether there will be enough like Mitch McConnell (or Mitt Romney or many others), we cannot yet tell. If the facts are foggy and the results are close enough to be within the margin of manipulation, the temptation to go along with that theft could well overwhelm integrity.

The purpose of the Electoral Count Act of 1887 was to guide Congress in the counting of electoral votes from the states. Since 1876, apart from Hawaii in 1960, there has never been a real issue about which slate of electors would be counted. But in 1887, there was no way to know that would be our future. The chaotic experience of a decade earlier, coming so soon after the end of a civil war, had seared into the nation's mind the catastrophic risk of states sending multiple slates of electors to Congress. The law therefore aimed to resolve the cases when Congress confronted multiple slates, by addressing every possible contingency. It was thus designed to deal with both the typical election and the extraordinary circumstances of 1876—that is, both cases in which a single slate of electors is presented to Congress and cases in which there are multiple slates presented, each purporting to represent the vote of the people.

If just one slate of electors was presented to Congress, the rules of the ECA looked (misleadingly) simple: section 6 described the procedure by which the governor (technically "the executive") lawfully certified a slate of electors; section 15 of the ECA then directed Congress that "no votes" from that slate "shall be rejected" *unless* both Houses "concurrently" conclude that those votes were not "regularly given." What "regularly given" meant was not explicitly defined, but the law was clearly speaking of the votes of the *electors,* not the votes of voters in the state's general election. Whether there were improprieties in the underlying popular election was not the issue the ECA addressed. If the governor lawfully certified the electors' appointments, the only question for Congress was whether the electors' votes were "regularly given."

So what would a nonregularly given vote be? Certainly, votes cast on a date other than the one designated by Congress as the day when the Electoral College meets would not be votes "regularly given." And certainly (we both think) votes shown to be the product of bribes, coercion, or some other delegitimating cause would not be votes "regularly given." There may have been other cases as well, such as a vote cast for a person not eligible to be president (because they are too young or because they are not a citizen, or—due to an obscure clause of the Fourteenth Amendment that has gained new prominence after January 6—because they have "engaged in insurrection"). But the text was clear that the focus is on *the votes of the elector,* not on the process by which the elector was appointed. This exception was not meant to swallow the whole of the ECA rule: there was no reason for Congress to set out the elaborate procedures of section 15 for determining properly appointed electors if it was reserving to Congress the power to reject a vote as not "regularly given" because Congress was troubled by the election triggering the appointment.

This was the easy case: a single slate, no contest about their appointment, certified by the governor. Let's call it "Case 0," as in the ordinary or default case.

Things got more complicated, however, if there was a contest about the slate of electors that should have been chosen (as in Florida in 2000) or if more than one slate of electors is presented to Congress (which, before 2020, except for Hawaii in 1960, never happened under the ECA). In this more difficult context, the statute imagines three possible scenarios: let's call them Case 1, Case 2, and Case 3.

The simplest of these more difficult cases—Case 1—was the procedure governed by the ECA's "safe harbor" provision in section 5. Under section 5, if a state had a procedure for resolving disputes about its election and that process was completed at least six days before the Electoral College was to vote, then that "determination" of which slate was the correct slate "shall be conclusive."

So, consider a hypothetical: if Pennsylvania had a procedure for contesting the results of a presidential election (in 2020, it did, including procedures such as a recount), and if that procedure was completed at least six days before the Electoral College was to vote (in 2020, it was), then, under section 5, the slate chosen by that procedure was the slate that represented Pennsylvania's electoral votes. The state's certification was "conclusive," as the statute says, and Congress had no power to recognize a different slate. (Remember this fact; it will be important below.)

Things get more difficult with Cases 2 and 3. Case 2 imagines two state officials who each purport to be the authorized authority for resolving a contested election (this is what happened in 1876, when different people claimed to speak on behalf of the state). In Case 3, there are competing slates in a state that has no authority qualified, at least in time, to conduct "judicial or other methods or procedure" for "final determination of any controversy or contest concerning the appointment of" electors. (Every state today has such an authority—a combination of administrative procedures including recounts and litigation in the state's courts. But it's easy to imagine that authority not completing its work "six days before" the Electoral College meets. Indeed, that's what happened in Wisconsin in 2020 because the election litigation in the state's courts did not conclude until several days after that deadline.)

We don't know of a case like Case 2 arising under the ECA. But for illustration, imagine that a state had both an administrative procedure for resolving contests about elections and a judicial procedure. Imagine that both represented themselves as the final certifying authority within the state and that these authorities disagreed about which was the proper slate under that state's law. In that case, the ECA called on the Joint Session to pick the slate determined to be the right one by the state authority that Congress believed was actually "authorized by [the state's] law." The Joint Session was to act, in other words, as a kind of judge between these two authorities, determining which, under that state's law, was to be the kingmaker.

Case 3 is easier to describe. Imagine that in 2000, the Supreme Court had not stopped the recount in Florida. (In the notes we explain exactly why, on the reasoning of the most conservative justices, the Court had no power to stop the recount.)[5] Imagine that the recount had resolved in favor of Al Gore and that the election board finally certified the state for Gore on December 30, 2000—fifteen days *after* the Electoral College vote. Imagine, finally, as in Hawaii in 1960, that both the Gore electors and the Bush electors had gathered on December 18, 2000, and cast their ballots for their respective candidates. In that scenario, under section 5, Congress would not have been committed to counting the Gore slate because Florida's resolution of the election dispute came too late. Under section 5, the Gore slate would not be "conclusive" because it was ultimately certified after "six days before" December 18. That is *not* to say, however, that the Gore slate couldn't be counted—as Wisconsin's slate in 2020 was counted, even though it had missed the "safe harbor" deadline, and Hawaii's slate in 1960, even though it, too, had missed the "safe harbor" deadline. It is only to say that the ECA did not purport to *require* Congress to count that slate.

Now that we've described the cases, what rules does the ECA provide for them? With Case 1, the rule was clear: under the "safe harbor" provision of section 5, the determination by a person or body with the authority to resolve any contest six days before the Electoral College votes was to be "conclusive" on Congress—so long as the electors' votes were "regularly given." Through the ECA, Congress had in effect promised the states that whatever happened in the states stayed in the states. The only question for Congress was whether the requisite state authority had certified an election result, whether it did so in time, and whether the votes of those electors were "regularly given." If Congress didn't think that there was one and only one undisputed state authority that resolved the dispute about which slate of electors was validly appointed and did so on time, then we're not in Case 1 at all—we're either in Case 2 (when there were multiple such purported determinations) or in Case 3 (when there were no such determinations), both of which we discuss below. If Congress recognized that the state's one and only authority for resolving disputes about electors reached a determination and did so on time, then the ECA bound Congress to count those electors' votes *unless* those electors' votes were not "regularly given." The ECA didn't explicitly say that Congress could concurrently reject votes not regularly given in Case 1, but we think it must have been implicit. There's no reason why Congress would have had the power to reject electors' votes procured by bribery or coercion in Case 0, where it is explicitly stated, but not in Case 1. In section 15's immensely convoluted text, we think that the statute's drafters simply overlooked including it in Case 1. The bottom line: in Case 1, Congress had to accept the state authority's slate, and it could reject those electors' votes only if both chambers concurrently decided that their votes were not "regularly given."

The rules for Cases 2 and 3 were just as clear, though the result was more uncertain. In both cases, the Joint Session was to choose among the competing slates. If both houses agreed on which slate was to be counted, that slate was counted. Critically, and again, in making its choice, Congress was not supposed to simply decide which slate it prefers. For Case 2, the Joint Session was supposed to determine which "State authority" was "the lawful tribunal of such State." Once Congress determined which authority was the state's "lawful tribunal," then it must count the "regularly given" votes cast by the electors "supported by the decision of such State so authorized by its law." In other words, Congress had to count the regularly given votes cast by electors that were "supported by the decision" of whichever state authority *Congress* thought was the state's "lawful tribunal." The question before Congress was about which *tribunal* was the state's legitimate one. Once it decided which tribunal spoke for the state, Congress had to accept the slate that this tribunal determined was the correct one.

For Case 3, because no state authority would have made a determination in time about which slate was valid, Congress couldn't defer to any state resolution of that question. So it had to address the question directly: it had to determine which slate represented the "lawful electors appointed in accordance with the laws of the State." The question before Congress again wasn't which slate it prefers or even whether there was voter fraud in the election. Every state has procedures such as recounts and administrative proceedings for resolving those questions. The question before Congress was which slate the state appointed pursuant to those laws. The ECA once again was calling on the Joint Session to act as a judge, not as a chooser.

With Cases 2 and 3, however, it is certainly possible that the houses would not have agreed. Even though the chambers were supposed to address the very same questions—which slate was "supported by the decision of such State so authorized by its law" (Case 2) or which represented the "lawful electors appointed in accordance with the laws of the State" (Case 3)—they might well arrive at different conclusions. Get a bunch of lawyers together and you're certain to find three answers for every two questions. And politicians who don't have to answer to a court are even more skilled at finding an argument that suits their political purposes.

So what would have happened if the two chambers did not agree?

Where there were multiple slates and none had received safe harbor certification (Case 2 or Case 3) and where the houses disagreed, then the slate certified by the governor was the one that counted. (The text of the ECA wasn't crystal clear about which cases the governor's tiebreaker applied to: it's clear that it applied at least to Case 3. We believe it logically must have applied to Case 2 as well, but we don't think it could have coherently applied to Case 1. The reason is that if the chambers disagree about whether there is a single state tribunal for resolving disputes, then we are automatically in Case 2.) Again—because this is critical—if there were multiple slates and Congress couldn't agree on which to count, the tie was broken by the governor. Call this the "governor's tiebreaker."

All this is complex, we know. We've tried to summarize it in a flowchart on the following pages. (Shaded boxes are implied.)

The basic structure should now be clear enough. The ECA wanted to give the states the primary authority to determine which slate of electors Congress would count. If the electors' votes were "regularly given" and the state sent just one certified slate, or if the state's unambiguous process for contesting elections resolved itself in time in favor of one certified slate, then that slate was the one Congress must count. But if there were multiple purported slates and the state didn't resolve the question on its own—either because there was more than one process for resolving contests about the vote or because there was no process that resolved the contest in time—only then did Congress have the power to select among competing slates. But Congress had to make that choice by applying state law: if there was more than one state authority purporting to resolve the dispute, then Congress had to determine which was the valid *authority* under state law. If there were no state authorities that resolved the dispute, then Congress had to determine itself which slate was appointed in accordance with state law.

In these narrow classes of failure, each house of Congress was to vote to decide which slate ultimately got counted—either directly in Case 2 or indirectly in Case 3 by deciding which state tribunal got to decide. Again, Congress was not supposed to pick the slate it preferred for political reasons. It was simply supposed to identify which slate the state had truly chosen according to its own laws. If the chambers agreed, the slate they agreed on got counted. If they didn't agree, then the slate with the governor's signature got counted.

We won't pretend that it's easy to parse the ECA. The statute was a mess. But as we entered the election of 2020, it was the law that we had. And in important respects, the key method for exploiting the law remains the same even after Congress reformed the law in 2022 through the Electoral Count Reform Act. So, the first question we should consider when thinking about 2025 is how well the ECA actually constrained the actions of Congress in 2021. If it worked well in 2021, we might have confidence in the ECRA. If it did not, then all bets are off. Either way, as the saying goes, hindsight is 20-20. (Sorry, we couldn't resist that one.)

Recall the facts of the election in 2020 as Congress *should* have seen them under the ECA: The governor of every state had sent Congress just one slate of electors. Those slates were properly certified under section 6 of the ECA. Except for Wisconsin (and maybe Georgia), all disputes within the states about who the lawfully appointed electors were had been resolved in time to satisfy the safe harbor provision of section 5. Therefore, under the plain language of section 15, Congress was instructed that "no electoral vote" from these fifty-one jurisdictions (including the District of Columbia) "shall be rejected"— unless the votes of *those electors* were not "regularly given."

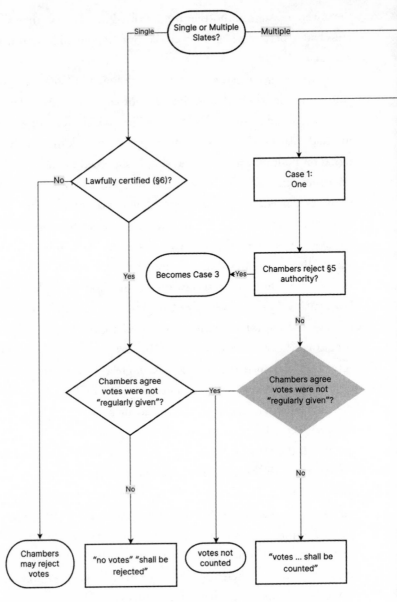

The (implied) logic of the Electoral Count Act

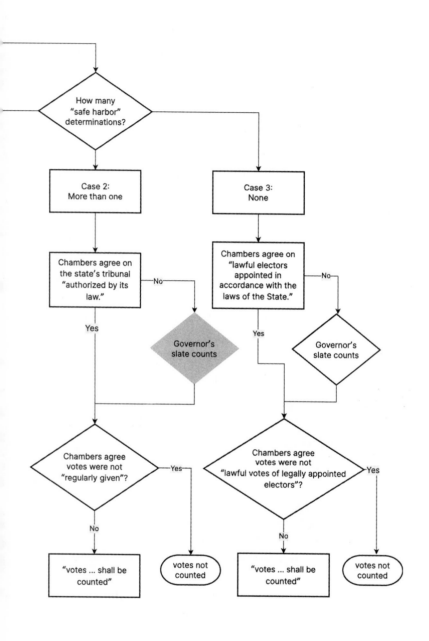

Obviously, those electoral votes were "regularly given." In none of the states did the electors vote on a day other than December 14, nor did anyone allege that any vote was not as it was intended, nor that President Biden was constitutionally ineligible to hold office. There was therefore no possible basis for the claim that any *elector's* vote was not "regularly given."

So then what about the objections made to the returns from Arizona and Pennsylvania on January 6? What were they about, and how did they fit into the ECA's legal framework?

Those objections were about the popular elections in those states, and so they didn't fit into the ECA's legal framework at all. Gaggles of elected representatives and senators in Congress took to the airways in the days before January 6, promising to challenge the election results on January 6. Senator Josh Hawley of Missouri—a Yale-educated lawyer, former law clerk to Chief Justice John Roberts, and former law professor at the University of Missouri—was the first and most prominent senator promising to challenge those results. His claim throughout was that there were problems in the *popular* election in those states. He never said that there was anything suspect about the votes cast in the Electoral College by the electors themselves. As he argued on the floor of the House on January 6, 2021:

> Let me just say . . . a word about Pennsylvania. . . .
>
> I say to Pennsylvania: Quite apart from allegations of any fraud, you have a State constitution that has been interpreted for over a century to say that there is no mail-in balloting permitted except for in very narrow circumstances, which is also provided for in the law. Yet, last year, Pennsylvania's elected officials passed a whole new law that allowed for universal mail-in balloting, and they did it, irregardless [*sic*] of what the Pennsylvania Constitution said.

Then, when Pennsylvania's citizens tried to be heard on this subject before the Pennsylvania Supreme Court, they were dismissed on grounds of procedure and timeliness, in violation of that Supreme Court's own precedent.

So the merits of the case have never been heard. The constitutionality of the statute, actually, has never been defended. I am not aware of any court that has passed on its constitutionality. I actually am not aware of anybody who has defended the constitutionality, and this was the statute that governed this last election in which there were over 2.5 million mail-in ballots in Pennsylvania.

This is my point: that this [house] is the forum. The Pennsylvania Supreme Court hasn't heard the case, and there is no other court to go to, to hear the case in the State, so this is the appropriate place for these concerns to be raised, which is why I have raised them here today.[6]

There are two problems with this embarrassingly ignorant argument by Missouri's law professor senator. First, Hawley was flat-out wrong about Pennsylvania law. As the Pennsylvania Supreme Court has expressly held, "We find no restriction in our Constitution on the General Assembly's ability to create universal mail-in voting."[7]

Second, and more important, *whether or not* the Pennsylvania courts were wrong about Pennsylvania law, the floor of the House on January 6 was absolutely not "the forum" for those questions to be resolved. And the reason it was not the forum is fundamental to the design of our Constitution and, especially, is fundamental to the principles of federalism. That design and those principles were, in turn, articulated and defended in the ECA.

Our Constitution gives each *state* the power to "direct" how its "Electors" are to be appointed. It then directs Congress to "count" the votes of the electors appointed by the states. The ECA was Congress's promise to "count" the votes of the electors appointed by the states, at least so long as those electors' votes are "regularly given." Without doubt, the Pennsylvania electors were "appointed" for Biden by the state of Pennsylvania. Without doubt, any contest about that appointment was resolved in time. Without doubt, their votes were "regularly given." And thus, without doubt, Congress was obligated to count the votes of the Pennsylvania electors, under the plain terms of the ECA.

Hawley's argument was that the Pennsylvania electors *should not* have been appointed, because on his allegedly "expert" (and erroneous) view of Pennsylvania law, the state should not have counted mail-in ballots. (Who knows how he knew what not counting the mail-in ballots would do for the ultimate results. We put that aside.)

But neither the Constitution nor the ECA gave Congress the power to decide whether electors *should have been* appointed. The only question under the ECA is whether they *were* appointed. If they were, and if their votes were "regularly given," then the ECA and the Constitution demand that Congress count those votes.

A hypothetical (not so far from reality) drawn from international relations might make this point clearer. In 2022, Jair Bolsonaro lost reelection as president of Brazil to the country's former president Luiz Inácio Lula da Silva, widely known simply as Lula. Inspired by Trump's antics in 2020, in the months before the Brazilian election Bolsonaro began spreading conspiracy theories about election fraud. After he lost by a small margin, he refused to concede defeat but—in a surprising relief to many who predicted he would remain in power through a military coup if necessary—left the country rather than violently resist Lula retaking power. Days after Lula's inauguration on January 1, 2023, Bolsonaro was photographed eating alone at a Kentucky Fried Chicken outside Orlando, Florida.

That bizarre but thankfully peaceful denouement did not last. On January 8, 2023, in Brasília—in a haunting echo of January 6,

2021, in Washington, D.C.—thousands of Bolsonaro's armed supporters stormed the country's congress, supreme court, and presidential offices inspired by the lie that Lula had stolen the election from him.

Now for the hypothetical part of our hypothetical: Imagine that Bolsonaro returned to Brazil and released a statement claiming that, as reelected president, he had appointed a new ambassador to the United States. The same day, Lula released a statement claiming that he, as newly elected president, had appointed a new ambassador to the United States. Both purported presidents' alleged ambassadors arrive in Washington, D.C. Which one of the two should President Biden receive as Brazil's ambassador to the United States?

The obvious answer is Lula's. Because he's the president of Brazil, he gets to appoint Brazil's ambassador to the United States. Unpacking the reasons behind that obvious answer helps to understand the ECA and Congress's role in counting electoral votes.

Our point is this: whether or not President Biden believed Bolsonaro's election lies—and they were lies, which President Biden, along with hundreds of other world leaders, has decisively rejected— it is simply not his role to decide who won Brazil's election for president. Like the United States, Brazil has a legal system that functions reasonably well, and that legal system concluded that Lula defeated Bolsonaro. That answer—Brazil's answer—is the only one that matters.

Senator Hawley's arguments on January 6, 2021, were as unmoored from the fundamental principles of federalism as our hypothetical Bolsonaro's arguments would have been in January 2023 from the basic concepts of international sovereignty. The ECA said to the Joint Session: if there is only one slate, and that slate is certified by the state, and no contest about that slate extended beyond six days before the Electoral College voted, then the *only* question for Congress is whether the vote of the electors was "regularly given."

Complaining about whether they *should* have been certified is like complaining that Brazil's legal system *shouldn't* have recognized Lula as the winner of Brazil's election.

Hawley ignored the plain instructions from the ECA and the Constitution. Instead, he thought it to be Congress's job to decide whether Biden or Trump legitimately won the popular election in Pennsylvania. Hawley and his fellow travelers claimed that fraud and other improprieties called into question whether Biden really got the most votes in the states they objected to. We don't think that assertion was factually right—none of the claims made in the sixty-three lawsuits filed in seven states raised issues that would have affected the results.[8] But *whether or not* it was factually right, the ECA was an expression of constitutional federalism: it was a promise to the states that Congress would count the votes from electors who were certified by the governor of that state *unless* those votes were not "regularly given." Yet here was a Yale-educated lawyer trying to rally his colleagues to reject the votes from Arizona and Pennsylvania when there was absolutely no basis for believing that those votes were not "regularly given."

What might Hawley say in his defense? (We tried to interview him for this book. Surprise! He refused.) Well, of course, if the ECA was unconstitutional, then maybe Congress is free to vote however it wants when counting electoral votes. But Hawley never made that claim when rallying for a revolution. Representative Louie Gohmert (R-TX) did in his lawsuit challenging the electoral process. And if indeed this 135-year-old law—which had governed more than half of the country's presidential elections—was unconstitutional, then all bets are off and we are back where the nation found itself in 1876. But we don't think that any court was going to find the ECA unconstitutional. And even if it were, the Constitution itself gives the power to appoint electors to *states* and reserves to Congress only the limited power to "count"—not to revisit or revise or second-guess—the votes of those state-appointed electors.

All this is meant to suggest that the real risk that we face in 2025 is not a risk in the law itself; the real risk is whether Congress will follow the law. There was no ambiguity under the ECA about what should have happened on January 6. That election presented the most straightforward cases under the ECA—single slates, certified by the governor, with any contested results resolved at least six days before the Electoral College voted (except, as we said, with Wisconsin). Yet 147 members in Congress flatly ignored the law on January 6, 2021. These 147 members stood to declare: we don't care what the law says, we are going to act to impede the free and fair election of the president of the United States. And the fact that 147 members in Congress could do that was not because of anything in the ECA. It was because 147 members of Congress either didn't know the law or didn't care.

This reality reveals the critical point: there's little reason to believe that Congress as an institution is under any real constraint because of the ECA or the ECRA. If members of the House and the Senate felt entitled to violate the clearest ECA command in the clearest possible case, how could any law hope to constrain them in more ambiguous cases? Remember that the ECA told members of Congress to recognize the slate that legitimately won the state's election, not simply to back the slate of their own party's candidate. But what prevents them from flouting that rule and voting on a purely partisan basis, perhaps wrapped in a fig leaf of pretext about whatever conspiracy theories they have fed their base?

Because that is exactly what happened in 2020. The objections raised in Congress did not even pretend to be about the electors' votes. They were formally phrased using the language from the ECA: that the "votes" were not "regularly given." But every argument marshaled to support the objections was about alleged fraud and illegality in the *popular* vote, not the *electors'* votes. On their face, the objections plainly violated the ECA. On their face, they were an embarrassment to the institution of Congress—and especially its most learned members, such as Missouri senator Josh Hawley.

And it gets even worse—because our challenge is not just willfully lawless senators and representatives. It is also the complete inability of our media to explain relatively complicated facts to a distracted and polarized public.

The election in 2020 was no exception. The media did a terrible job pressing the dissenting representatives on the precise question that would have shown the lawlessness. Every interview quickly devolved into the irrelevant debate about whether the claims of voter fraud had been adequately investigated or adjudicated at the state level. Here's an exchange between one of the most qualified journalists to comment on the matter, George Stephanopoulos, and Senator Rand Paul:

STEPHANOPOULOS: To begin with the threshold question for you, this election was not stolen. Do you accept that fact?

PAUL: Well, what I would say is that the debate over whether or not there was [election] fraud should occur. We never had any presentation in court where we actually looked at the evidence. Most of the cases were thrown out for lack of standing, which is a procedural way of not actually hearing the question. There were several states in which the law was changed by the secretary of state and not the state legislature. To me, those are clearly unconstitutional. And I think there's still a chance that those actually do finally work their way up to the Supreme Court. Courts traditionally and historically don't like to hear election questions. But yes: Were there people who voted twice? Were there dead people who voted, were there illegal aliens who voted? Yes. And we should get to the bottom of it. . . .

STEPHANOPOULOS: Senator Paul, I have to stop you there. No election is perfect. But there were 86 [*sic*] challenges filed by President Trump and his allies in court. All were dismissed. Every state certified the results: [garbled] after investigation, counts, and recounts. The Department of Justice led by William Barr said there's no widespread evidence of fraud. Can't you just say the words "this election was not stolen"?

PAUL: What I would suggest is that if we want greater confidence in our elections, and 75 percent of Republicans agree with me, is that we do need to look at election integrity. And we do need to see if we can restore confidence in the elections.[9]

Yet those questions were precisely *irrelevant* under the ECA (as Senator Paul conceded when later in the interview he acknowledged that it would have been wrong to vote to overturn the results). Whatever happened in the election in the state of Pennsylvania, the ECA promised that where there was only one slate of electors certified under section 6—"no [such] electoral votes" that were "regularly given" "shall be rejected." Yet Senators Hawley, Ted Cruz (R-TX), and others were rallying Republicans to "reject" those votes—without that lawlessness even being named by the very best in the media.

The experience of 2020 presses a fundamental question about what kind of law the ECA was and what kind of law the ECRA now is. Ordinarily, laws can be enforced. We can imagine a court either penalizing some person or institution for violating the law or ordering them, through an injunction, to obey the law. Defiance, ordinarily, carries consequences.

Yet it's almost impossible to imagine a court imposing consequences under the ECA or ECRA. In Cases 0 and 1, the ECA directed that electoral votes not "be rejected" on the grounds that the objectors pressed on January 6, 2021. But Josh Hawley is not going to jail for lawlessly defying the plain language of the ECA. And if he had succeeded in getting Congress to reject the electoral votes of Arizona or Pennsylvania, no court was going to reverse that decision or order Congress to count its votes differently. The reasons for this reach deep into theories—which we need not explore here—about the proper scope of judicial power. Suffice it to say that the ECA could not compel Congress to act in ways Congress doesn't want to act. And that precisely is the problem with any law that purports to regulate how Congress must behave—including the ECRA, the ECA's replacement.

Instead, the ECA acted more like the rules governing each house (and the Joint Session on January 6) than an external constraint imposed on Congress by a separate legal authority with enforcement power over Congress. Seen this way, the law clearly set the default for how electoral votes would be counted. But if both houses decided to do so, those defaults could be cast aside. This is the law of New Year's resolutions: binding until ignored, and if ignored, then ignored without consequence. Congress is free, on this understanding, to construct its own reality with its vote. And that constructed reality can be based on conspiracy theories of voter fraud that (contrary to the ECA's text) empower Congress to reject electoral votes. No other institution can check it in that construction. Congress is a law upon itself.

The filibuster rules of the Senate provide a useful comparison that illuminates the reality-defying logic of these sorts of self-binding rules. Under the current rules of the Senate, if any senator raises an objection to the taking up and debating of (almost) any bill, the rules require proponents of the bill to rally sixty votes before debate on that bill can proceed. (Certain legislation is exempted from this "rule," such as budget resolutions and judicial nominations.) This is why Senator Kyrsten Sinema (I-AZ) calls it the "sixty-vote threshold."

As Senator Michael Bennet (D-CO) describes in his wonderful book *The Land of Flickering Lights* (2019), that rule might seem perfectly clear. Sixty is a whole number. Even lawyers can count to sixty. Yet in practice, the rule turns out to be not so clear at all.

The actual filibuster rule works like this: If a senator calls on Congress to take up a bill for Senate consideration, and even just one senator objects, the Senate must take a vote. If only fifty-nine senators vote to take up the bill, the plain meaning of the "rule" is that the bill cannot be taken up. Fifty-nine is not sixty; the "sixty-vote threshold" requires sixty votes. The president of the Senate would thus be instructed by the Senate parliamentarian that fifty-nine is less than sixty and that therefore the bill cannot be taken up for a vote.

Yet that ruling by the parliamentarian can itself be appealed to the Senate. That is, any senator is free to challenge the parliamentarian's ruling that fifty-nine is less than sixty by making a motion on the floor of the Senate calling on the Senate to concur in or reject the parliamentarian's decision. That appeal is then decided—*by a simple majority vote.* And so, in a truly Orwellian sense, after an appeal has been raised, the Senate president will ask the Senate whether the Senate—by a simple majority vote—agrees that the sixty-vote threshold has not been met, because only fifty-nine senators have voted to proceed. If fifty-one senators vote to overrule the parliamentarian (or fifty, with the vice president casting the deciding vote), then the ruling of the chair—that fifty-nine is less than sixty—is overruled. By majority vote, Congress is free to decide that up is down, left is right, and that fifty-nine is greater than or equal to sixty. There is no legal check on that decision. The Senate's rules are not subject to external judicial enforcement.

The same is true about the ECA. Yes, the ECA told Congress what it must do in every case and did so most clearly in Case 0: if the votes of the electors are "regularly given," those votes shall "not be rejected." But Congress was as free to ignore that requirement as the Senate is free to declare that "fifty-nine" is "sixty." And this fact points to the first of the two critical stress points in our system for electing the president under the ECA or the ECRA. If both houses of Congress are controlled by the same party, then in principle, that party can do as it wishes. Even in Case 0, when there is only a single slate, if both houses are controlled by the same party, they could flout the ECA and reject the certified votes of that slate. Congress can't—in a stronger or more formal sense, at least—cast its own electoral votes. If it rejects a slate and there's no other slate for Congress to count, that means that the state has lost its vote for president. But whatever the reality—one slate or many, and if many, one slate certified by the governor—a rogue Congress can ultimately do as it pleases. And although 2020 gives us hope when the vote is clear, in the fog of a closer election, we cannot be sure.

The events of 2021 show the importance of that qualification—that *in practice* Congress can do as it pleases. On January 6, Republicans in the House and Senate challenged the certification of electoral votes from Arizona and Pennsylvania. As we have described, had Mike Pence rejected the certified results and accepted the votes of the alternative slates, his decision would have been appealed to the Joint Session. Under the rules governing the Joint Session, each house would have gathered on its own and voted on whether to overrule Pence's decision. Clearly the House, controlled by Democrats, would have voted to overrule him. But the Senate was still controlled by the Republicans. So *had they chosen to,* those Republicans could have voted to affirm Pence's ruling and thereby reelected Donald Trump.

But that perfect unanimity among Republican senators, while theoretically possible, crashed on the shores of perhaps rare political integrity. The Republicans in the Senate were fifty separate individuals. Leader McConnell rejected the challenge to the electoral votes, and even if he hadn't, it's clear that enough Republicans would have defected from any effort to overrule any state's certification of its electors. A powerful faction of the Republican Party might have favored it, but the real question was whether enough Republican senators would have gone along. The answer—at least in 2020—was no.

The conditions surrounding the election in 2024, however, could well be different. The margin in the Electoral College could be smaller. The results in swing states could be closer. The claims of fraud could be made to look more plausible. The political energy supporting an effort to reverse the results could be greater. And if politicians could see the goal line, and if it seemed to be within easy reach, they could well become bolder in seeking to cross it.

Here, then, is how the ECA would have enabled that crossing. Rather than constraining Congress, the ECA was better described as an enabler for rogues in Congress. Many members may refuse to restrain themselves by the rules expressed in that law, especially when those rules are complex or hard to discern. And if the plain language of the rules gives them an opening to get what they want, they're very likely to point to those rules to defend their actions. Relatively clear *procedural* rules about how electoral votes were to be accepted or rejected provided a road map that Congress can travel. But the obscure *substantive* rules about the grounds on which Congress was supposed to base its votes—for example, whether the electors' votes were "regularly given" but not whether there was alleged fraud in the state's election—were no constraint at all.

Once we recognize that the ECA established a framework for the legal impact of each chamber's vote without constraining the substance of those votes, we can see the most important destabilizing feature of the ECRA: the incentive it created for rogue governors.

In our hypothetical, a MAGA Republican has become the governor of North Carolina. During the campaign, they promised to "defend North Carolina voters" against voter fraud and intimidation. After the election, they become convinced that the MAGA Republican candidate for president won the popular vote—if "properly tallied," according to them—in North Carolina. They therefore resolve to do whatever they can do to assure that North Carolina's electoral votes get cast for the MAGA Republican.

This is a governor going rogue. A rogue governor is the greatest threat to the system under both the ECA and the ECRA.

Under the ECA, the strategy would have been deceptively simple: a rogue governor could have stolen the election just by certifying, under section 6 of the ECA, the slate of electors for the MAGA Republican—regardless of how the state had voted. In every election, the governor receives the results from the state election administrators, certified under state law by those officials in favor of the candidate who won the state's election. But in this scenario, the governor asserts that those results are wrong. The misinformation environment of social media and the balkanized world of legacy media, in which partisan voters hear only their side's propaganda, creates fertile ground for the governor to make unsubstantiated claims of fraud. Based on those claims, the governor certifies the results under section 6 for the challenging candidate—the MAGA Republican, even though that candidate legitimately lost the vote in North Carolina.

The Biden team would then have challenged the North Carolina governor's decision to certify the results for the MAGA Republican. Under the ECA, a court may or may not have ordered the governor to certify differently. The tradition in America has been that the governor's certification—like the vice president in the counting of electoral votes—is merely ministerial. They are not to decide anything substantive about the results. Their job is simply to sign a certificate reflecting the decision made by the voters, as determined by the state's legal processes for administering elections. But our hypothetical imagines that the governor asserts that fraud has infected the results in certain districts. They therefore discard the results from those districts and recalculate the results accordingly. Now the MAGA Republican has "won" the state, the rogue governor certifies, and those certificates are sent to Washington.

Under the original ECA, things could have gone one of two ways: Congress might have considered only the governor-certified MAGA Republican slate, or it might have considered both the governor-certified MAGA Republican slate and the uncertified-but-legitimate Biden slate. Either way, under the original ECA, Biden would have faced an enormous challenge.

First, consider the case when Congress considered only the governor-certified MAGA Republican slate. How might that happen, given that the Biden electors legitimately won the state's election? The problem was that if the rogue governor doesn't certify the Biden electors, it's possible that no one else could. The plain language of section 15 suggests that some other state official, or even the Biden electors themselves (as the "alternative" Trump electors from several states did in 2020), should be able to send their own slate to Congress. Remember, section 15 said that the vice president was to present "all the certificates and papers *purporting* to be certificates of the electoral votes." But in 2021, the parliamentarian ruled (wrongly, in our view) that only certificates satisfying the requirements of section 6—slates that have been certified by the governor—can be presented to Congress. That's why Congress never considered the fake Trump electors in 2021. Of course, that decision might be reversed in 2025—Biden would have the benefit of Vice President Kamala Harris presiding over the Joint Session. But if the parliamentarian's ruling from 2021 stands, the only slate that would have come before Congress under the ECA would have been the MAGA Republican slate.

In this scenario, where Congress considers only a single slate that was lawfully certified by a rogue governor, the ECA commanded that Congress "shall [not] . . . reject" that slate's electoral votes as long as they were "regularly given." If Democrats followed this command, then Congress would not reject the slate sent in by the rogue governor. And with that, the rogue governor could steal the election for the MAGA Republican—and shockingly, they could have done it *through* the procedures of the ECA, not by defying them.

What if Democrats *didn't* acquiesce to the rogue governor's certified slate? What if they argued that the certification in these circumstances was not "lawful," because the governor issued it in violation of state law?[10] In that case, the Democrats might claim, with some justice, that the MAGA Republican slate was not "lawfully certified" and vote to reject it on that basis. Maybe they would have argued, with moral if perhaps not legal force, that the bogus certification of the MAGA Republican's electors broke the system so badly that they were forced to use whatever levers of power they could grasp to save our democracy. Constitutional hardball begets constitutional hardball.

Here's where the ECA's flawed structure would have combined with the allocation of political power to create truly catastrophic risks. Remember that when Congress receives just one slate from a state, the ECA requires that it count that slate's electoral votes *unless both chambers vote to reject it*. So if a Republican-controlled Senate voted to accept the single governor-certified slate, then the rogue governor's slate gets counted *no matter what the Democrats did*. If the political pieces had fallen into place like this, then Republicans could have stolen the presidency for the MAGA Republican—and under the ECA, Democrats would be powerless to stop it.

But what if, in our hypothetical for 2025, Congress considered both the governor-certified MAGA Republican slate and the uncertified-but-legitimate Biden slate under the ECA? That is, what if Vice President Harris ruled that the Biden slate could be presented to Congress (because it "purports" to be a certificate of electoral votes), so that Congress would have before it both slates of electors? You might think that this would improve the Democrats' hand, because at least Congress would be considering the legitimate Biden slate alongside the bogus MAGA Republican electors. But under the ECA, with the two houses controlled by two different parties, this ultimately would have changed nothing.

With both purported slates before it, Congress would have to choose between them. Both Democrats and Republicans could marshal arguments in favor of their candidate's slate. The Biden camp could insist that the Biden electors should be given "safe harbor" protections because they were certified by the state's highest court as the winner of the election, and section 5 promises "safe harbor" to "judicial . . . procedures." (This is Case 1 from above.) But the MAGA Republican's allies could argue that North Carolina law gave its governor, or its Republican legislature, the power to resolve matters finally. Then there would be two purported authorities claiming section 5 "safe harbor" (Case 2). In the face of that impasse, one might think that there wasn't any "final determination" of the dispute by the state—after all, the dispute rages on (Case 3). The ECA doesn't provide separate procedures for determining whether Congress is facing Case 1, Case 2, or Case 3.

The statutory text of the original ECA becomes nearly impenetrable at this point. But remember that the law's substantive rules didn't really constrain Congress at all, though its procedural rules might. So the immensely complicated substantive rules of the ECA in practice actually boiled down to two simple procedural rules. If there was only one slate before Congress, then Congress counted those electors' votes unless both chambers voted to reject them. If there were multiple slates before Congress, then Congress picked which slate to count—and if the chambers disagreed about which slate to count, then it had to count the governor's slate.

In our hypothetical, this means that if the chambers disagreed about which slate to count, then the tie is resolved in favor of our rogue North Carolina governor. And that in turn would mean that regardless of whether both slates are presented to Congress, the original ECA gave the rogue governor enormous power. No matter what, the governor's slate counted unless *both* chambers voted to reject it.

Call this the "rogue governor's gambit" under the ECA. And although 2020 saw no governor take it—and the elections in 2022 saw none of the candidates who promised to take it prevail—its threat was reason enough to amend the ECA.

That, thankfully, is what Congress did in late December 2022. The Electoral Count Reform Act had been inspired by the debacle of January 6, 2021. And it was designed, in part, to avoid the rogue governor threat.

Yet though the ECRA makes the rogue governor's gambit less likely, it does not eliminate it. No doubt it is an improvement. But interestingly, the improvements in the ECRA that have attracted the most attention turn out to be the least important.

The most talked about change in the ECRA is that it clarifies that the vice president's role on January 6 is merely ministerial. Of course, we agree as a matter of constitutional law, and it's of course a good thing that the statute books reflect a correct view of the Constitution. But Eastman's theory was that the *Constitution* endowed the vice president with the power to reject electoral votes—not the ECA. And if the Constitution does in fact give the vice president such power, a statute passed by Congress can't take it away—just like Congress can't revoke a pardon by the president, because it is the Constitution that expressly gives the president that power. As we've argued, we don't believe the Constitution gave the vice president any power to resolve disputes in the electoral count. But the point here is this: the ECRA can't change whether the vice president has that power or not. Its most prominent reform is thus legally inert.

The ECRA also raises the threshold for an objection triggering debate in Congress. The ECA had given a single senator and a single member of the House the power to object to a state's electoral votes, as long as they put their objection in writing. The ECRA raises that threshold to 20 percent of both chambers. That's certainly a sensible change, because it avoids political grandstanding by members like Senator Hawley, raising fringe and lawless objections that have no hope of being accepted by Congress. Such grandstanding can undermine the country's acceptance of the finality of elections by giving the false impression that the outcome was truly in doubt. And as we saw on January 6, 2021, that false impression can lead to tragically violent consequences.

But raising the objection threshold can *never*, as a matter of logical certainty, make a difference to the outcome under the ECRA. As we will explain below, the ECRA provides a simpler rule than the ECA: Congress can reject the governor's certificate only with a concurrent vote of *both* houses. (If this sounds catastrophically vulnerable to the rogue governor's gambit, put that thought on hold for a moment.) As a result, for an objection to make a difference in the outcome, it needs the support of at least 50 percent of both chambers—more than enough to clear both the ECRA's new 20 percent objection threshold and the ECA's old low threshold of a single member of each house. So raising the threshold will never block an objection that would have ultimately passed both chambers.

Yet there are two truly important changes in the ECRA. (We'll discuss the first now and the second in the next chapter.) These two changes were meant to eliminate any risk created by the law regulating the electoral vote count. Unfortunately, they both fail to do that. In this chapter, we'll look at how it fails where there is a rogue governor and an extremely close election.

The first change directly targets the rogue governor strategy. The new system works as follows: Just as under the ECA, the state's governor is responsible for certifying the state's slate of electors. But to avoid the risk of multiple slates, the ECRA adds a critical check on the governor's certification. If the governor certifies the wrong slate, an "aggrieved candidate" may sue in federal court to challenge the governor's certification. If the court agrees with the "aggrieved candidate," then the ECRA directs Congress to treat the certificate "as required to be revised by any . . . judicial relief" as conclusive. Thus, if the governor issues a bogus certification, and the legitimate winner successfully sues in federal court to get it corrected, Congress must follow the court and not the rogue governor.

But here begins the first critical ambiguity in the new ECRA—and no matter which way this ambiguity is resolved, it creates real problems under the statute.

Imagine with our hypothetical that our newly elected North Carolina governor declares that they will not certify the Biden electors. Instead, they certify the slate of MAGA Republican electors. This certification is wrong, under the facts as our hypothetical lays them out. How does the ECRA remedy that wrong?

The assumption of the drafters was that Biden would go to court and ask the court to tell our rogue North Carolina governor to certify the correct slate: the Biden slate. Imagine that the court does that. But imagine that now the governor refuses. "A federal court has no business telling me which slate of electors I'm going to certify. The Constitution gives to the states the power to select their electors. I've certified the slate I believe is correct. That's all the certifying I'm doing."

One way of reading the statute suggests that the court could do no more than use all the powers it has to enforce its judgment against the governor—including the power of criminal contempt. You might think that the threat of jail is an adequate incentive to ensure that the governor complies. After all, what greater threat can the law wield?

But recent history illustrates the weakness in that logic. Several years ago, a federal court in Arizona jailed Maricopa County sheriff Joe Arpaio for his continued defiance of its order to stop violating federal civil rights statutes in his treatment of immigrants and minorities. President Trump pardoned Arpaio, who immediately walked free. A recalcitrant governor who certifies a bogus slate and defies a court order to change the certification *in order to install their preferred candidate as president* can count on that candidate pardoning them once taking office. And the governor's bogus slate gets counted in Congress unless *both* houses vote to reject it.

Call this the "recalcitrant rogue governor's gambit" under the ECRA. The ECRA raises the stakes considerably compared to the ECA, but a governor who is willing to risk jail for a month or two can steal their state's electoral votes. That might seem extreme, but imagine if Kari Lake in Arizona or Doug Mastriano in Pennsylvania—two deeply committed election deniers—had won their races for governor. Is it really that implausible that these politicians, who supported the January 6 insurrection and have called its violent perpetrators "political prisoners," would be willing to spend a few nights in jail themselves for the cause? And the same with our hypothetical new governor in North Carolina: how better to catapult themselves to MAGA hero status than going to jail for a few months to support the president?

This possibility raises the questions: Why does the governor need to sign the alternative certificate at all, if the court has ruled that the alternative is in fact the correct slate? Why isn't the court's ruling enough on its own?

And indeed, the language of the statute could support this reading. Section 5(c)(1)(B) of the statute says that "[a]ny certificate of ascertainment of appointment of electors *required to be issued* or revised by any [court] shall replace and supersede" the governor's certificate (emphasis added). The language "required to be issued" could refer to that certificate whether the governor has obeyed the order of the court and signed the correct certificate or not. This way of reading the statute would therefore give the court's ruling effect whether or not the governor complied with it.

But this interpretation just creates a different problem. Now there would be two slates of electors: one being the slate wrongly certified by the governor, and the other the slate that the court directs should have been certified. We can presume that the electors behind both slates gathered and voted on the day the law requires; the record of the votes from each slate will then be presented to the vice president on January 6, 2025. But now, under section 15 of the ECRA, the vice president is directed to "open the certificates and *papers purporting to be certificates* of the votes of electors appointed pursuant to a certificate of ascertainment of appointment of electors issued pursuant to section 5." There are, in our hypothetical, two such "certificates and papers purporting to be certificates." One is the certificate signed by the governor; the other is the certificate that should have been signed by the governor, along with a court order declaring this to be the proper certificate. Which does the Joint Session count?

The ECRA does not resolve that conflict. The essence of its design was to avoid the possibility of multiple certificates. But as we've shown, the statute actually fails to avoid that possibility. More directly, our hypothetical shows that there *is* the possibility of multiple certificates—at least under one interpretation of the ECRA. If the governor is recalcitrant, then either the Joint Session has just one certificate before it—the wrong one—or it has two certificates before it, with no mechanism in the ECRA to deal with multiple certificates beyond the statutory declaration that one "supersedes" another. The ECRA specifies two and only two permissible grounds for objecting to those votes: (1) whether the certificate naming the electors was "lawfully certified" by the governor, potentially as revised by a court; and

(2) whether the electors' votes were "regularly given." If Congress has both certificates before it, it could reject the one the recalcitrant governor signed (finding it not "lawfully certified"), but only if *both* houses vote to support the objection. If the houses can't agree on either, then conceivably both certificates would be before the Joint Session, presenting the impossibility that both are to be counted. No doubt, if good faith rules, the Joint Session can work it out. But the whole question motivating this book is what happens when we can't count on good faith prevailing.

The recalcitrant governor is not the only possible bad actor under the ECRA. Ironically, despite its attempts to minimize the role of the presiding officer to merely ministerial tasks, the ECRA also gives the vice president a way to wreak havoc. On January 6, the ECRA directs the vice president to open all the votes "purporting" to be cast by electors certified by the governor. Suppose that the governor certifies the right slate. But then suppose that the vice president ignores that certification and instead opens the votes cast by the electors of the vice president's party. The only recourse under the ECRA is for members of Congress to object to counting those votes and for both houses to sustain that objection.

This recourse is insufficient for two reasons. First, if just one of the two houses goes along with the plot, then the objection fails, and the vice president's sleight of hand is successful. And the hyperpartisan House of Representatives might do just that. Second, even if the objection succeeds, the ECRA has no procedural mechanism to count the *right* slate if the vice president doesn't recognize it first. All Congress can do is reject the *wrong* slate.

That half remedy permits the plot to succeed in a close election by depopulating the Electoral College. Imagine that Vice President Al Gore had attempted this move in 2000 and that the ECRA had already been law. He could have opened the Gore electors' votes for

Florida instead of the Bush electors' votes. Let's say that Congress did the right thing and objected to those electoral votes, so they weren't counted. But Bush's electoral votes in Florida wouldn't be counted either. So the total number of electors appointed would be reduced by Florida's 25 electoral votes. Of the remaining 513, Gore would have won a 51.9 percent majority with 266. And with it the presidency.

Call this the "vice president's sleight of hand." Simply by opening the bogus slate of electors on January 6, the vice president can make it difficult for Congress to reject those bogus electoral votes. And if the election is close enough, they can steal the presidency even if the objection succeeds. Kamala Harris is exceptionally unlikely to attempt this strategy on January 6, 2025. A future vice president might not be so loyal to the rule of law.

Finally, the ECRA still gives Congress its own way to reverse the results: like the ECA, the ECRA enables Congress to reject the votes of electors from a state that produces a single slate of electors only if both houses vote to do so. (Unlike the ECA, the ECRA never contemplates multiple slate scenarios—as we have explained, in theory at least, it's the governor's slate or nothing.) And like the ECA, the ECRA doesn't define the terms it provides as the grounds for objection: that the electors were not "lawfully certified" and that their votes were not "regularly given." As we saw in 2021, the law's relatively clear procedural rules (and the integrity of key actors in the Senate) as a practical matter bound Congress—because flouting them would be too obviously lawless. But its more obscure substantive rules about the permissible bases for those objections did not bind Congress at all. So, as in 2021, members of Congress in the future could object to electoral votes by claiming they are not "regularly given" while citing conspiracy theories about voter fraud. It's just Josh Hawley 2.0.

Call this "the congressional override." Because there is no enforcement mechanism outside Congress—such as a court—that binds it to respect the ECRA's limits on proper bases for objection, those limits bind Congress only to the extent that it chooses to be so bound. And because the ECRA's grounds for objection retain the ECA's opaque and antiquated terminology, the political constraints on Congress respecting those limits are weak. Not invisible—again, they were weaker in 2021—but the clarity of the result tied to the integrity of key senators meant that the result would not be flipped. But under the ECRA, if the results are not clear, we can't say what will happen. The temptation to do wrong will be significant, especially if bolstered (as in 1876) with serious claims of voter fraud or intimidation.

Because the ECRA empowers Congress to reject the governor's electoral votes only by a vote of both houses, this is a less pressing threat than manipulation by a recalcitrant governor or by the vice president. Realistically, the Senate is unlikely to go rogue even if the House will. But our point is simply that if it does, the law as it is provides no real way to stop it.

Our bottom line is this: Under the ECA, rogue governors represented a catastrophic threat that was the most potent strategy that could be used to steal a presidential election. The ECRA goes a long way to disarming that threat by making it much harder for a governor to persist in submitting a spurious slate. But the reform is incomplete. As it stands, the ECRA enables recalcitrant rogue governors, a vice president's sleight of hand, and an overriding Congress to steal a state's electoral votes.

Of these three potential risks, we fear the recalcitrant rogue governor much more than a vice president's sleight of hand or an overriding house of Congress. The return from political opportunism is greatest with a governor, costliest with a vice president, and most diffuse with Congress. But with all three, the risk is directly tied to how clear the results from the election were: if it is as it was in 2020, charges of a stolen election notwithstanding, the risks are much less than if it is as close as it was in 2000. Or put differently, the closer the result, the greater the incentive of each to act against it.

---

tl;dr

The strategy: In the context of a close and contested election, a recalcitrant rogue governor intervenes to certify a slate of electors contrary to the apparent popular vote.

The chance that this strategy flips the results in 2025: moderate

The chance that this strategy flips results in future elections: high

Summary why: The ECRA requires Congress to count the slate of electors certified by the governor unless both houses of Congress vote to reject it. Thus, a rogue governor and the House can together steal the state's electoral votes. In a close contest in the Electoral College, they can steal the presidency. The ECRA gives courts the power to override the governor's decision. But the mechanisms for enforcing that override are weak and inconclusive.

The strategy: The vice president, while presiding over the Joint Session of Congress on January 6, opens a bogus slate of electors instead of the slate certified by the governor.

The chance that this strategy flips the results in 2025: minimal

The chance that this strategy flips results in future elections: high

Summary why: The ECRA directs the vice president to open the votes "purporting" to be cast by electors certified by the governor. But Congress can overcome the vice president's decision to instead open a bogus slate only by a vote of both houses.

The strategy: Congress votes to reject a state's legitimate electoral votes, claiming that the electors are not "lawfully certified" or that the electors' votes were not "regularly given."

The chance that this strategy flips the results in 2025: minimal

The chance that this strategy flips results in future elections: moderate

Summary why: The ECRA limits the grounds for Congress rejecting electoral votes, but it does not define the terms it uses.

6

The "Force Majeure" Game

In Georgia in 2020, there were two races for the United States Senate. That's unusual. Senators are elected for six-year terms, but in each state the terms are staggered. Yet because of the early retirement of Senator Johnny Isakson in 2019, Senator Kelly Loeffler had been serving a shortened term—under state law, just until the next election, rather than the entire remainder of his term. She was appointed to the Senate on January 6, 2020, and had to run for reelection the next fall. One race in Georgia was thus between Loeffler, a Republican, and the Reverend Raphael Warnock, a Democrat. In the other Senate race, Democrat Jon Ossoff ran against a Republican incumbent, David Perdue.

No candidate in either race received a majority of the votes in the election in November 2020. Under Georgia law, this meant that there had to be a runoff election. On January 5, 2021, to the great surprise of many (including both of us), both Democrats beat their incumbent Republican opponents. Only four other times in American history had both of a state's Senate seats flipped in the same election.[1]

Elections don't ordinarily happen as they do in Georgia. In practically every other jurisdiction in the United States, the person who gets the most votes wins the election, whether they win a majority or not. (Alaska and Maine are the exceptions.) In one of our own congressional districts, MA-4, in 2020, nine candidates were vying for the

Democratic nomination (which, because the district is heavily Democratic, effectively also meant the election). The winner received just 22.4 percent of the vote—which means that 77.6 percent of Democrats didn't support the ultimate nominee. Georgia's sensible policy assures that the winner must be a candidate that a majority at least finds acceptable, even if that person is not most people's first choice. (An even more sensible policy would be to hold the run-off at the same time as the election, using a "ranked-choice voting" method. Alaska and Maine do that.)

Georgia's policy, though now an outlier, is not new. Nor has it always been limited to candidates for Senate. At various times from the founding through the Civil War, three states—Massachusetts, New Hampshire, and Georgia—required that presidential electors receive a majority of votes cast to be appointed. A mere plurality, all that any state now requires in a presidential election, was not enough. If the initial election didn't yield a majority winner, then the state had to take further steps to pick the electors.

Those states' majority requirements didn't matter much at the time. For the first handful of elections, states varied widely in their systems for selecting electors. Article II, section 1, clause 4 of the Constitution gives Congress the power to determine when states may appoint electors. At first, Congress gave the states a lot of time to appoint their electors: states could appoint electors at any time within the thirty-four days preceding the first Wednesday in December of each presidential election year.[2] States complied with that requirement in a variety of ways. Some states gave the choice to their legislature; some gave the choice to the people by a popular vote, either statewide or by congressional district. And some conditioned the people's right to choose electors on whether the people had voted by a majority: if they had, their choice was the choice of the state; if they hadn't, the state legislature would choose.

By allowing states to choose electors over thirty-four days, Congress had created an obvious incentive to cheat. Many did. In the 1840s, parties engaged in "pipe-laying"—the transporting of voters from one state to another to cast votes in multiple states, taking advantage of the different days on which the states held their popular elections.[3] That problem led Congress in 1845 to decide that the appointment of electors must happen on a single day. Congress didn't (and couldn't, under the Electors Clause of Article II of the Constitution) tell states *how* they should appoint electors. But it could, and did, require that however they appointed electors, they had to do so "on the Tuesday next after the first Monday in November, in every fourth year succeeding every election of a President and Vice President." Thus was Election Day born.

This rule created a problem for states—such as Georgia, Massachusetts, and New Hampshire—that had majority vote requirements.[4] If the voters in such a state didn't pick a candidate by a majority vote on Election Day, then the election on that day could not be said to have "appointed" a slate of electors. (Ranked-choice voting was invented in Europe in the nineteenth century but not used in the United States until the 1920s.) And if that's the only day on which the state has the power to appoint electors, then that state would either have to give up its majority requirement or not be represented in the Electoral College.

The problem was obvious at the time Congress passed the legislation establishing Election Day—at least to the members of Congress from those states. When Ohio Democrat Alexander Duncan introduced a proposal for selecting a single day on which electors could be appointed, New Hampshire congressman John Hale immediately noted that it would create problems for states like his, which might not be able to select candidates on a single day if that selection required a majority vote. Duncan then suggested an amendment to his proposal, to allow that "when any State shall have held an election for the purpose of choosing electors and shall fail to make a choice on the day aforesaid, then the electors may be appointed on a subsequent day, in such manner as the State shall, by law, provide."[5]

This provision, codified as 3 USC § 2 until the ECRA repealed it, would give a state such as New Hampshire the power to specify "by law" how electors are to be chosen if the election doesn't produce a majority winner. The new provision still didn't tell states how to appoint their electors if the timing exception applied. Perhaps some states would, like Georgia, hold run-off elections in the legislature, while others would have their legislatures appoint the electors.[6] But in historical context, "fail to make a choice" refers specifically to the contingency created by states that might require a majority vote to win an election. More generally, we think it points to any condition imposed by law before an election that determines whether an election has made a choice. Thus a state could say that a candidate must receive 60 percent of the vote to win. If no candidate did, that election would "fail." Or it could say that an election is valid only if 50 percent of eligible voters cast a ballot. An election with 40 percent turnout, on that view, would "fail." The key on this understanding is not just the word "fail" but "failed to make a choice." That refers, as Joshua Matz has argued to us, to a standard that is or is not met on Election Day.[7] It does not, however, refer to any inability to figure out what had actually happened on Election Day. (Here's a nice law school hypothetical: What if lightning strikes the building in which all the votes have been collected? Does the election "fail" even though an omniscient observer knows who received the most votes?)

Legal scholars have disputed this narrow view of section 2, arguing for a slightly broader interpretation. Professor Michael Morley notes that immediately after Hale pointed to the problem caused by the method his state used for choosing electors, Representative Samuel Chilton pointed to a different problem in his own state, Virginia. There, elections for president were by voice vote, and Chilton worried that weather might prevent voters from assembling on the appointed day. Virginia law thus permitted the board of elections in each district to extend the election if a significant number of voters could not show up. Chilton worried that the flexibility the voice vote system required would be prohibited by the new federal law.[8]

Under Morley's view of the 1845 law, Congress accommodated both Virginia's and New Hampshire's concerns. And by reading those two as within the scope of "fail to make a choice," Morley's interpretation opens up other contingencies that might also qualify. What if there's a natural disaster, such as an earthquake? Or a dangerous weather condition, such as a hurricane, that prevents thousands or even millions of people from reaching the polls? If, as Chilton said of Virginia, weather made it impossible for most to participate in the vote, could the state argue that the election had "failed" on Election Day?

Morley argues yes. But while Chilton's remark provides support for that view, there are also reasons to doubt it. Michael L. Rosin offers two considerations that point the other way. First, Congress rejected efforts to broaden the exception even more. And second, Virginia subsequently changed its law to conform to the less permissive federal standard. As an original matter, we find Rosin's points persuasive. If Congress had accommodated Virginia's concern, there would have been no reason for Virginia to change how it conducted its elections immediately after the new law was passed.[9]

Either way, if we go by how Congress understood section 2 when it enacted it, there is only a small range of "fail[ures]" that remain on the interpretive table: either Rosin's view that it covers just mathematical requirements such as a majority winner or Morley's slightly broader view that covers those cases plus natural disasters. A little fuzzy no doubt, but not much of a risk to the electoral process over-all. The range of possibilities is either one extremely narrow exception or two extremely narrow exceptions.

Yet that scholarly dispute about the original meaning of the 1845 law is really beside the point. The real risk that the original section 2 created was caused by something that might seem weird about the way statutes are read today: whatever the original understanding of the word "fail," it is not obvious that courts today would restrict a state legislature to that original understanding.

You might wonder how the word could mean anything different from what it meant in 1845. How could its meaning change if Con-gress has not changed the text of the statute?

That question has an intuitive answer and a legal answer. Intui-tively, the phrase "fail to make a choice" might seem, in the eyes of someone living in the twenty-first century, to embrace much more than the numerical technicality that first motivated it. Even the broader conception that might include weather and natural disasters doesn't cover situations that, to the modern ear, might also sound like a "fail." Consider a terrorist attack, which actually did disrupt an elec-tion on 9/11: New York City was scheduled to hold the primaries for its mayoral election that day. After the planes hit the Twin Towers, the city postponed the primaries for two weeks, and votes that had been cast on 9/11 weren't counted. Might that, too, count as an elec-tion that had "failed"?

Legally, statutory interpretation increasingly lives by strict rules that mirror this intuition. Even if a word or phrase in a statute was never intended by its drafters to apply in a particular way, the plain meaning of the words might nonetheless cover that application. Take the case of Title VII, the law enacted in 1964 to address workplace discrimination. Title VII bans "discrimination" "because of such indi-vidual's . . . sex." The paradigm case was clear: Congress, in 1964, was focused on workplace rules that prevented women from participating equally in the workplace. It was not focused on discrimination against transgender individuals. Transgender individuals have existed since ancient times, but societal recognition of their existence and of their civil rights has lagged millennia behind the movement for equality among cis-gendered men and women. Had you asked a member of Congress in 1964 whether the law was intended to protect the transgendered, they would almost certainly have said "no."

But in 2020, the Supreme Court upheld the application of the law to transgendered individuals.[10] By a 6–3 vote, in an opinion authored by conservative justice Neil Gorsuch, the Court held that the plain meaning of the terms applied to transgendered individuals, even if no one would have imagined it when the law was passed. "Textualist interpretive methods direct attention to the original meaning of the statutory language," as Joshua Matz has put it, "though this differs from a hunt for original expectations about how that language would apply in particular cases."[11]

If the original meaning of "fail"—or of "failed to make a choice"—controlled its modern meaning, in the sense that the phrase covered only what its drafters intended it to cover, then the original section 2 would not have been much of a danger. No state today requires a majority vote for presidential electors or sets conditions on the success of an election beyond one candidate getting more votes than the others. Even the broader sense that might encompass natural disasters imposes important practical limits. After all, it's hard to fake an earthquake.

Yet if that original intended scope didn't set the boundaries of section 2's application, then the law opened up the process to a state legislature blatantly manipulating the outcome of an election after the fact.

This game would have been simple: the state holds a popular election on Election Day. But if the state legislature doesn't like the outcome, it drums up a pretext—phantom allegations of voter fraud are the obvious one—to declare that the state "failed to make a choice" on Election Day. Politicians would probably succeed in convincing much of the public that the broader, revisionist conception applies because, original meaning aside, the vague phrase is malleable to the modern ear. And even if the courts reviewed the issue, contemporary statutory interpretation doctrine might be stretched to bless the legislature's game. Armed with that expansive legal power ("the electors may be appointed on a subsequent day in such a manner as the legislature of such State may direct"), the state legislature then picks the electors it prefers. Game over.

Indeed, the state at the center of our hypothetical—North Carolina—teed this possibility up after the election of 2000. In 2001, North Carolina passed a law to assure that the state would be represented by presidential electors regardless of what happened in an election—including a protracted legal battle that ran up against constitutional deadlines, as had just happened in Florida.[12] The first section of the law gave the legislature the power to pick presidential electors "whenever the appointment of any Presidential Elector has not been proclaimed" by the "safe harbor" deadline set out in the ECA. The second section gives the governor the power to pick presidential electors if "the appointment of any Presidential Elector has not been proclaimed" by noon the day before presidential electors are to vote. The law thus gave the state legislature the first crack at appointing electors, and if it hadn't done so by a few days later, the governor got that power. In both cases, the appointer was to "designate Electors in accord with their best judgment of the will of the electorate." What was the check on that exercise of "judgment"? Nothing. "The judgment itself," the law instructed, "of what was the will of the electorate is not subject to judicial review."

Texas did something similar. In 2001, Texas amended its constitution to give the governor the power to "convene the Legislature in special session to appoint presidential electors if the Governor determines that a reasonable likelihood exists that a final determination of the appointment of electors will not occur before the deadline prescribed by law to ascertain a conclusive determination of the appointment."[13] Here again, the state was trying to exploit the permission it thought was given to it by the original section 2 of the ECA.

We believe that both laws were plainly inconsistent with section 2 of the ECA. Section 1 of the ECA required states to appoint their electors on Election Day. Then section 2 created a limited exception to that requirement, permitting each state to appoint electors on a later date *only if* it has "fail[ed] to make a choice" on Election Day. But as we've explained, "fail[ed] to make a choice" had a specific meaning. It didn't mean "the choice is not yet known." It meant that literally, under the rules as they were, no choice had been made *at all*. Texas's and North Carolina's laws abused that exception, by authorizing the state legislature or governor to appoint electors, not because a choice hadn't been made, but because they didn't know yet what that choice was. They hadn't finished counting the votes (and resolving any contests about that count). This is not the exception section 2 allowed.

Neither law was ever challenged because neither was used. Both could well have caused havoc. By giving the legislature or the governor the power to appoint electors who, in their unreviewable opinion, reflect the will of the people, simply because of a delay in counting or resolving an election dispute, the law created an obvious incentive to skew the results. There are a million ways to slow the process of resolving an election contest. And while courts can try to move things along, courts don't always have the power or the will to do so. A strategic effort to stall the process of deciding an election could shift that decision from the people to the legislature or the governor.

In North Carolina, there is a further twist: the delay strategy could make sense for either political party. In 2020, the North Carolina legislature was controlled by Republicans. But at the time the presidential electors are selected, the legislature is not ordinarily in session. To call it back into session would require a supermajority (three-fifths) vote by the legislature. This means that Democrats could have blocked that vote as long as they had two-fifths of the legislature. Because the legislature wouldn't be in session, it couldn't appoint electors under the law, leaving the decision to the governor—who, in 2020, happened to be a Democrat and in 2024 will be a Democrat again. These sorts of quirks in state law compounded the opportunity for, and danger of, strategic games. Had North Carolina been a determinative state in 2020, there would have been a huge incentive for both sides to try to play this game.

All this shows why it was crucial for Congress to address the problems with section 2. And here again, thankfully, Congress did. As with the governor's gambit discussed in the last chapter, Congress addressed the problem in the Electoral Count Reform Act. But as with the governor's gambit, unfortunately, the ECRA is only partially successful in disarming this dangerous game.

Congress could have addressed the section 2 problem in the ECRA in several ways. One would have been to abolish section 2 completely. There's not much need for section 2 as originally intended: to the extent that a state wanted to assure a majority vote in its presidential election, ranked-choice voting (in use by Maine and Alaska) is a perfectly acceptable alternative. And it's reasonable to think that the danger of election subversion posed by spurious invocations of the exception outweighs the flexibility that exception offers in the rare case of a natural disaster.

Congress didn't follow this strategy. It instead opted for an alternative fix: remove the word "fail" from the statute completely but then try to specify more clearly the kinds of problems that entitle the state to appoint its electors after Election Day. Natural disasters are easy to include, harder to define. (Is a severe rainstorm enough to trigger the exception? What if that severe rainstorm happened in West Palm Beach in 2000, when an additional few hundred voters making it to the polls could have changed the result?) Insufficiently reliable voting technologies, by contrast, should not be included at all: Congress should never give states an incentive to have poorly functioning election technology. Allowing an election to be delayed, or the decision made by a legislature, because of a freak ice storm is different from shifting power to a strategic political actor because results were "uncertain."

Unfortunately, Congress didn't specify a list of situations in which the exception applies. The ECRA could have listed, for example, "natural disasters, terrorist attacks, or other similar catastrophes." Instead, the statute simply says that a state may "modify the period of voting" if "necessitated by force majeure events that are extraordinary and catastrophic, as provided under laws of the State enacted prior to such day." But what are "force majeure events that are extraordinary and catastrophic"? Do phantom allegations of voter fraud qualify? The law doesn't say. And compounding the problem, the law doesn't require that a federal court have the final say about what counts as a force majeure event. Opportunistic state politicians might still have the final say.

Congress did, however, get one important thing right in the ECRA's changes to the section 2 exception: if the exception applies, it no longer permits the state legislature or governor to appoint electors. Instead, all the state can do is extend the period of voting. That makes a great deal of sense because that's all that's needed if voting is interrupted by a hurricane or a terrorist attack. If polling in the state is dramatically disrupted on Election Day, then the state can hold an emergency makeup election. If New York City could do that two weeks after 9/11, any state can do it. This substantially reduces the incentive for a state to invoke the exception strategically. Extending the voting period might give the losing candidate's supporters more time to cast their ballots, but it doesn't permit the state legislature to substitute its will for the people's.

Overall, the ECRA has done enormous good to remove the threat of the section 2 game. Although a partisan legislature or governor could invoke the force majeure clause to continue balloting, they cannot use the old section 2 to substitute their choice for the choice of the people. The ECRA thus renders North Carolina's and Texas's laws no longer effective. After the ECRA, there is no congressional authority for a state legislature selecting a slate of electors merely because the results are not finalized before either the "safe harbor" provision or the date the Electoral College votes. If a state hasn't resolved the election before the Electoral College votes, then, as with Hawaii in 1960, both slates of electors can gather to cast their ballots. Assuming, as with Hawaii, that the contest is resolved before January 6, the prevailing side will have its votes counted. And if it doesn't resolve the contest before January 6, then, as with New York in 1789, its electoral votes will not be counted.

All this underscores a critical point that too many forget: without statutory authority, there is no way for a state to appoint its electors after Election Day. Although the Constitution clearly gives the states the power to select the "manner" by which electors are appointed, it also clearly gives Congress the power to say *when* electors are to be appointed. Congress has done that: Election Day, *except* if a force majeure event justifies continuing the election after Election Day. Beyond that one exception, there is no possibility for a state to appoint a new slate of electors, regardless of whether the state would be represented in the Electoral College.

There is one lingering opportunity for gamesmanship. A state can no longer, under any circumstances, empower the state legislature (or the governor or anyone else) to directly appoint electors after Election Day. But that doesn't eliminate the moral hazard. Suppose in the days after Election Day, a MAGA Republican state legislature sees that the state's popular election will yield an extremely close victory for the Democratic candidate. At that point, it has nothing to lose by declaring that a force majeure event has happened—probably invoking phantom allegations of voter fraud—thus giving MAGA voters more time to cast their ballots. Of course, if the MAGA candidate won the votes cast by Election Day, the state legislature would see no need to extend the voting. Heads the MAGA Republican wins; tails we let more people vote. That strategic second bite at the apple is possible precisely because the ECRA isn't specific enough in defining a force majeure event and doesn't explicitly require a federal court to determine that such an event has actually happened. So here we see again that, as in the preceding chapter, the ECRA's work is not yet finished.

One final hypothetical, given to us by the writers of the extraordinary HBO series *Succession*, shows this final problem most clearly. (Spoiler alert! If you've not finished season 4, skip to the tl;dr!)

In the penultimate episode of season 4, there's a presidential election. The results are extremely close, and the contest would be decided by Wisconsin. But in Wisconsin, a fire breaks out at a Milwaukee polling place, destroying a large number of presumptively Democratic ballots. Because of the lost ballots, the state is called for the Republican.

How would that case be decided under the ECRA?

Not very well, it turns out. The ECRA would give Wisconsin officials the right to extend voting to address the loss. But it would not require it, nor would it authorize a federal court to order it. So the (Republican) legislature could well decide to do nothing, leaving the selection of the Republican electors, even though Democrats would have won the state had there been no fire.

That result is certainly not reassuring—especially now that this episode (and idea) is out in the world!

---

tl;dr

The old strategy: Using section 2, give political actors the power to declare the election as they determine, because the election was not resolved quickly enough or on the basis of unsubstantiated claims of election fraud.

The chance that this strategy flips the results in 2025: significant

The chance that this strategy flips results in future elections: significant

Summary why: The law creates an opportunity and incentive for state politicians to manufacture a "failed" election so that they can replace the results of the popular vote with their own choice of electors.

The new strategy: Using the Electoral Count Reform Act's force majeure exception to Election Day, a state legislature gives the losing candidate's supporters a second bite at the apple.

The chance that this strategy flips the results in 2025: moderate

The chance that this strategy flips results in future elections: moderate

Summary why: The law allows a state to extend the voting period in an election, but the law still gives the legislature discretion. If a force majeure event occurs, the legislature can choose whether or not to extend voting, depending on how it views the likely outcome of more voting.

7

Who's the Judge?

More than four hundred years of American experience with the ideal of democracy—yes, there was democracy in America before the Revolution—has evolved a relatively stable conception about the distinction between applying the law and making it. The more you study law, the harder it is to sustain this difference. But to Americans freed of the burden of a law school education, it is clear that there are people who make the rules and other people who apply them.

The clearest example of this distinction is "courts" versus "legislatures." Congress gets to make the laws it wants—with the approval of the president (unless it overrides a veto) and within the constraints of the Constitution. So, too, with state legislatures, constrained by governors and by both the federal and state constitutions. But courts are supposed to do what the law requires—if indeed the law is clear enough to require anything. The legislature gets to say, "If you embezzle cryptocurrencies, you will be fined ten times the value you embezzled." The courts are supposed to apply that penalty to people the criminal justice system finds guilty of embezzling cryptocurrencies. Courts are not to decide to exempt such people from punishment or to impose a penalty of fifty times the amount embezzled. Those judgments are for the legislature.

The difference between voters and the people who count the votes is another example of this intuitive but ultimately elusive distinction. As voters, we're free to cast our ballots as we wish, on whatever basis we like. We might be drawn to the candidate's policies, their eloquence, who we'd trust in a crisis, or who we'd like to grab a beer with. But the people who count the votes are not supposed to make a choice based on their own political preferences. They are supposed to be reckoning the choice made by voters. We all understand that those tabulators will have to make judgment calls and that some of those calls will be close—remember Florida's hanging chads! But the basic premise is that the process should have integrity. Regardless of the outcome, those determining the outcome should do so without regard to their own political preferences. To paraphrase Chief Justice John Roberts, they should be umpires calling balls and strikes rather than players on one team or the other.

The election of 2020 gave us some impressive examples of this integrity, maybe none more so than what happened in Georgia. Georgia is a profoundly Republican state—at least when you look at its state government. Governor Brian Kemp is a Republican. Georgia's secretary of state Brad Raffensperger is a Republican. Both were vocal supporters of President Donald Trump and strongly expressed the hope that he would win the election in 2020. But when the vote tallies indicated that Trump had not won their state, these two Republicans stuck to the truth. Even when Trump apparently tried to persuade Raffensperger to alter the results—"I just want to find 11,780 votes"—Raffensperger would not give in.[1] The votes had been counted correctly, these Trump-supporting Republicans insisted, and they were not going to be bullied into "finding" enough votes to flip those results.

Similar examples multiplied across the nation. Arizona's Republican governor, Doug Ducey, refused to be bullied by the president. And though Pennsylvania, Wisconsin, and Michigan all had Democratic governors, their Republican legislatures refused to take instruction from the Trump campaign about how they could try to flip the results leading up to (or even after) January 6, if the legislature stepped in and took control of their electors. (There were individual state legislators across the country, including in these states, who tried to do Trump's bidding. But no state legislature was remotely close to taking any official action.)

Some critics point to such examples to argue that people like us should just chill. If even Donald Trump couldn't persuade election officials to flip the results in 2020, why should we worry about the next time—especially when things went so poorly for MAGA Republicans in 2022?

But as we've said, we are pretty chill (as Lessig's fourteen-year-old would put it) about a clear election or an election in which the results can't be doubted without departing too dramatically from reality, as in 2020. However, the hypothetical we're considering is an election that is not so clear, where the results are very close and claims of fraud or intimidation are everywhere. The risks we're evaluating are in that context, not the context of 2020.

The election of 2022 does give us hope. No doubt, the strategy that Steve Bannon had hatched—for populating the ranks of election administration with people willing to "defend the truth"—did not succeed. Bannon's army was not to be filled with Raffenspergers or Kemps. It was to be an army of activists keen to produce a particular result—regardless of the votes of the people they are duty-bound to respect.

We don't mean to suggest that these partisans intend to purposefully steal an election they know a MAGA candidate lost. That might be true about Bannon, but not necessarily of his acolytes. The truth is more dangerous—and much sadder. Millions of Americans actually believe the Big Lie—that Democrats stole the election from Trump in 2020—and they believe that Democrats will steal it "again" in 2024.

For Bannon's strategy to work, these people need only believe the delusion that they are defending against another "theft" of an election. The phantom "stealing" against which MAGA Republican partisans would imagine themselves defending might take the form of rejecting legitimate vote tabulations on the basis of conspiracy theories of voter fraud. Or it might be a blunter tit for tat: because Democrats will steal the election in 2024, Republicans must preemptively steal it better. Wrongs, in this moral logic, beget justified wrongs, at least in the mind of the wrongdoer. At a rally in Arizona in January 2022, Trump himself used the alleged theft by Democrats to justify Republicans' doing the same.[2]

Yet as bad as that sounds, there is an even more worrisome risk to the integrity of those who decide election results. The second reason we should not be complacent about the election in 2024 is a potential corruption even more insidious than stocking the ranks of election workers with partisans committed to conspiracy theories. And this corruption may well be the most effective way to assure that the election produces the results the MAGA wing of the Republican Party seeks: redefining who is the ultimate judge of elections.

This strategy is to name the state legislature itself as the final elections board. In doing so, the legislature itself would replace the process formerly administered and judged with integrity by independent public servants. The process would begin just as it does now: people would vote, and those votes would be counted by election administrators. But the final tallies would be presented to the legislature acting as an elections board. The legislature would then either affirm the results as presented or overrule them. Either way, the decision would become a judgment about whether, in the view of the legislature, the results accurately reflect the will of the people. But unlike the public servants who (thus far) have performed that function honestly and without partisan favor, this hybrid legislature/elections board could—and, in our world of constitutional hardball, arguably would—"decide" the election results in favor of its party's candidate.

This idea is not as crazy as it sounds. Texas has already done something close to it. The Texas Constitution gives the governor "exclusive jurisdiction of a contest of the election of presidential electors."[3] And we came very close to this reality in 2000.

As we've described, in 2000 the election turned on the results in Florida. Both sides believed they had prevailed, and both sides fought to enforce the rules they thought would show that they had prevailed. The Gore campaign pressed for recounts. The Bush campaign pressed to stop the recounts. Remarkably, postelection analysis showed that both campaigns were wrong about the best strategy for assuring their own victory. If the recounts had extended to where the Bush campaign wanted them to, Gore would have won. If the recounts had been limited to the districts Gore requested, Bush would have won. Strategic wisdom is hard in the fog of legal and political war.

The fight for a recount came to a head when the Florida Supreme Court ordered a recount of some but not all counties. The Bush campaign complained about that selectivity, charging that the court was cherry-picking the counties that were likely to favor Gore. The United States Supreme Court took the extraordinary step of stopping the recount altogether while it heard arguments about the counting procedures. Then, after hearing the arguments and agreeing that there was a problem in the procedure outlined by the Florida Supreme Court, the Court declared that the selective recount was indeed unconstitutional. But alas, a majority of the Court concluded, there was no time for a more complete recount. Florida law indicated, at least the Court said, that the state wanted the advantage of the "safe harbor" provision of section 5. Any recount would certainly delay the results until after that "safe harbor" date.[4] The results had to stand as they were. George W. Bush was thus selected by a margin of just 537 votes.

All that is familiar history. What's less familiar is a move that would have made John Eastman famous twenty years earlier. While the campaigns' lawyers were litigating the actual election, another tactic was brewing in the Florida state legislature. In part at Eastman's behest, the legislature was considering a resolution to simply declare the election for Bush and appoint to the Electoral College the twenty-five Republican electors.

As we explained in the last chapter, that would have been illegal— at least if the Florida legislature was simply acting to choose a slate of electors after Election Day. The Constitution expressly gives to Congress the power to say when electors are appointed. Congress had exercised that power, and in 2000 the states were required to appoint their electors *on* November 7. The Florida legislature therefore had no power to appoint electors *after* November 7. The resolution purporting to do that therefore should have had no legal force.

This conclusion is resisted by people who believe in what's called the "independent state legislature theory," or ISLT. That theory has received increasing attention in recent years, both before and after the election of 2020. In 2023, the Supreme Court considered one version of the argument in the case *Moore v. Harper.* The North Carolina Supreme Court held that the congressional districts set by the state legislature were so extremely gerrymandered that they violated the North Carolina Constitution's guarantee of "free" and "fair" elections. The North Carolina legislature argued that this amounts to the state judiciary, rather than the state legislature, determining the "manner" of congressional elections.

The ISLT lay at the foundation of the plan advanced by Eastman and others for state legislatures to submit "alternative" slates of electors to Congress in advance of January 6, 2021. Any version of the ISLT that suggests that this strategy was constitutionally sound is wildly incorrect. But because the ISLT has gained currency among Trump partisans, and because several Supreme Court justices have signaled support for a weak version of the theory, it warrants a brief digression.

The ISLT comes in many flavors. Its essence is that because the Constitution gives state legislatures the power to select the "manner" by which electors are chosen, no other branch of the state government (the courts or the executive) or even the state constitution may alter or constrain what the legislature does. That position is controversial enough. More controversially, the theory seems to hold that it is federal courts that must determine whether the state legislature's laws are being complied with. A state court cannot decide the matter, because any such decision would amount to the state court usurping the power that the Constitution assigns to the state legislature.

The ISLT has been under attack since it was hinted at by Chief Justice William Rehnquist in his concurrence in *Bush v. Gore*. We think that Akhil Amar and Vikram Amar have planted the final stake against it.[5] In its narrowest form, the theory might hold that the legislature's power to set the manner of choosing electors cannot be constrained by anything save the federal Constitution. This narrow version is what was at issue in *Moore v. Harper*.

That view finds support in parallel aspects of the federal Constitution. For example, the Supreme Court has twice held that state law can't constrain the freedom of a state legislature to determine whether to ratify an amendment to the Constitution—because the power to amend is given by the Constitution directly to the state legislature. That precedent might no longer be sound; *Chiafalo* can be read to undermine this "immunity from state control" interpretation of the federal Constitution. The federal Constitution created the office of presidential electors. Yet *Chiafalo* holds that the states can regulate those electors.

The Court ultimately rejected even this weak version of the ISLT, to our great relief. But two important loopholes linger. First, a legal loophole. Although the Court said that state constitutions and state courts constrain state legislatures, it also said that there is a fuzzy limit to that constraint. Without adopting a clear rule for the future, it said that "state courts may not transgress the ordinary bounds of judicial review such that they arrogate to themselves the power vested in state legislatures to regulate federal elections."[6] Whether that exception is small or swallows the rule will play out in 2024. Second, a political loophole. After the North Carolina Supreme Court's initial decision in *Moore* striking down the state legislature's map, there was a judicial election. Republicans retook control of the state supreme court. Once they did, the court overruled its prior decision, holding that the North Carolina Constitution doesn't prevent the state legislature from gerrymandering after all. This highlights a key issue to which we will return. The Supreme Court's decision in *Moore* says that state courts *can* constrain state legislatures, but it does not say that they *must*. Because most state supreme courts are politically controlled—either through political appointment or even through direct election of the justices—there is a risk that state courts won't ultimately provide the safeguard that *Moore* says they can.

Nonetheless, whatever the merits of the weak form of the ISLT that the Court rejected, it could never have justified a state legislature's direct appointment of electors after Election Day, as Trump and his allies pushed in 2020. The weak form of the theory merely says that the state legislature gets to decide *how* electors are appointed, unconstrained by (for example) state courts or the state constitution. But it says nothing about *when* a state may appoint electors. And anything beyond this most narrow view of the ISLT is fatally weak.

Remember that the Constitution gives Congress, not the states (or their legislatures), the power to set the time for appointing electors. As a result, the ISLT cannot empower the legislature to appoint electors at a time other than the time described by Congress. As clear as it is that the state legislature has a power granted by the Constitution, so, too, is it clear that Congress has a related power granted by the Constitution. Even if the ISLT is right, no state legislature can have the power to appoint electors on a day other than the day Congress has said. The ISLT would not have justified the Florida legislature appointing electors after the election in 2000. Nor would it have permitted a state legislature to appoint electors after Election Day in 2020 (or after January 6, 2021—or even, as some constitutionally illiterate people have suggested, after President Biden was inaugurated on January 20, 2021).

The ISLT therefore does not create the risk that a state legislature will reverse the results of the state's popular vote by appointing electors after the fact. (It does contribute to a different risk, which we will discuss in the final chapter.) Yet there is a way that a state legislature could de facto accomplish that late appointment.

Imagine that Florida reworked its law just a bit. Rather than the Elections Canvassing Commission judging the validity of the results, imagine that Florida law said that the Florida state legislature itself judged the validity of the results. The vote tallies would be collected and reconciled and then presented to the legislature as the ultimate judge of elections. The legislature would then vote on whether to accept the result as the true expression of the people's will or to reject the result because the legislature believes (or pretends to believe) that the reported result does not express the people's will. In the majority of the legislature's view, their party's candidate "really" won.

Could they do this? The Constitution gives the states the power to decide how electors will be chosen. Early in the nation's history, some state legislatures chose electors directly. Over time they have ceded that power to the people, as determined through the peoples' votes. But there is no federal constitutional obligation to keep the cession absolute or unmixed. It would not violate the text of the Electors Clause of Article II for a state to decide that its legislature must oversee that process. Supporters of such a move might argue that reviewing election results is a political judgment perfectly suited to a political body such as the legislature. We disagree, because politicians—unlike nonpartisan election officials and courts—have no particular expertise at counting ballots or resolving legal disputes. And to return to a theme that threads through this book, politicians cannot avoid being biased in deciding election results. But regardless, we are not the Supreme Court. And absent unprecedented legal arguments that have never been tested in court, nothing in the Constitution requires that the people making political decisions be free of bias.

And because the state legislature would declare itself the *final* election board for presidential elections, its determination of who won the most votes on Election Day would be unreviewable by state courts. As Akhil Amar has noted, this strategy would work at least within limits—it couldn't be *too* dramatically detached from reality.[7] The state legislature's decision must follow *federal* law. That means it must comply with 3 USC § 1, which requires that states appoint their electors on Election Day and not later (as long as the force majeure exception we discussed in the last chapter doesn't apply). Given that every state's election board reaches its final decision days or even weeks later, you might wonder how states ever comply with the rule in 3 USC § 1 that the choice of electors be made on Election Day. The key, as we explained in chapter 6, is the difference between when a decision was *made* and when we *discover* what it was. Election Day is the last day on which votes may be cast. An omniscient God would know who won as soon as the polls closed; we mortals need more time to work things out. So long as the working out is viewed as determining what happened on Election Day, it is consistent with the command of section 1. The electors were appointed on Election Day; but it takes time to determine who they are. But if a state legislature, in its role as final election board, departs too much from what happened on Election Day, then a court could find that it has crossed the line from discerning which electors were appointed by the popular vote into belatedly—and unlawfully—appointing those electors itself.

That the state legislature's determination is subject to federal law also means that it must comply with the Constitution. If the legislature's decision was too radically arbitrary, the Supreme Court might decide that it violated the Equal Protection Clause—the provision the court relied on in *Bush v. Gore,* which held that a state "may not, by later arbitrary and disparate treatment, value one person's vote over that of another's." One might think that this principle is violated by a state legislature that tosses the reported results of an election based on conspiracy theories about fraud.

There might also be an argument based on the Due Process Clause. Though the case law is only suggestive, we think that such a challenge to this arrangement would have significant strength. An election is a commitment to a determination by the people. Adding a political actor at the apex of that determination conflicts with the principle of elections. That's not to say that the Due Process Clause would limit a state's ability to choose the electors itself. (We'll consider that possibility in the next chapter.) But it is to say that a process intended to determine which candidate was in fact selected on a particular day, but that then adds a political actor at the last stage, unnecessarily weakens that determination.

Where do these arguments leave us? If a legislature—such as Florida's in 2000—looks at the results as reported by canvassing boards and decides that it believes the board counted the votes improperly or included certain votes improperly, the legislature could plausibly assert that when properly reckoned, the voters chose a different candidate from the one presented by the canvassing boards.

If the results were close enough, that claim would be hard to reject. But if the results were clear—if the margin were wide and sustained by clear evidence—then the legislature's reversal after the election could violate the Constitution.

Making the state legislature the judge of elections would thus give significant power to the party in control to decide who won an election. That is an enormously dangerous power. As we will discuss in the next chapter, the Constitution permits state legislatures to appoint electors directly. But they may do so only by establishing, in advance, direct appointment as the state's "manner" of choosing electors. The strategy in this chapter is more insidious. It allows a state to hold a popular election and then enables the legislature to substitute its preferred candidate under the guise of announcing the result. The state can thus pretend to have a democracy when in reality the results are preordained by those in power. This is a common strategy in authoritarian pseudo-democracies. And as long as the state legislature doesn't depart too far from reality, it is almost certainly legal in the United States.

---

tl;dr

The strategy: Make state legislatures the final judge of election results.

The chance that this strategy flips the results in 2025: high.

The chance that this strategy flips results in future elections: high.

---

continued

Summary why: No constitutional requirement likely forces separation of the legislature from the process of determining the results of an election. Giving the legislature the power to "judge" elections could give them the power to flip the results regardless of the actual vote.

8

The Nuclear Option: Back to the Founding

For many years, Republicans have criticized America's administration of elections. They have insisted for decades that elections across the country are marred by widespread voter fraud. In response to those allegations—never sustained with any solid empirical evidence—they have implemented techniques to remove voters from the voting rolls and to restrict access to voting. We won't name the motives for these efforts. We can only affirm the result: in the year after President Biden took office in 2021, eighteen states passed thirty-four voting restriction laws. Many of these new laws became possible because the Supreme Court's decision in 2013 in *Shelby County v. Holder* struck down key provisions of the Voting Rights Act. Every one of the laws passed the state legislature on a party-line vote. Although the precise partisan effects of these laws will emerge only over time, the fear is that those laws will disproportionately disenfranchise demographics that tend to vote Democratic.[1]

That longtime trend culminated in 2020 with the most extreme rhetoric in a presidential campaign that the nation has seen in modern times. President Trump insisted again and again that the election was stolen. For a moment, before January 6, the wind seemed to have gone out of those sails. And for about forty-eight hours after January 6, the nation's leaders seemed united in the view that the president had gone too far and that Trump had not been denied office illegally. But in a demonstration of his continued control over the party, the former president pressed his claim that the election had been stolen. And after polls confirmed that most Republican voters agreed with the president, most Republicans in Congress closed ranks behind him.

Because of these actions, much of America stands convinced that many of the states can't count votes accurately: that our system for running our democracy is as fundamentally flawed as anything the government does—which, for many Americans, means that it is a complete and corrupt failure.

This link should not be overlooked. For the past forty years, it has been the Republican Party line to disparage government in all its capacities (except, of course, its capacity to wage war or police violent crime). Even the Federal Bureau of Investigation has come into Republicans' crosshairs due to its investigations of Trump. Bureaucrats are painted as lazy and incompetent; agencies that do important work with limited resources are framed as the Deep State, enemies of the people. No doubt, the fact that we don't fund the general welfare at a level appropriate for a nation as prosperous as ours makes some of those claims of ineffectiveness plausible. And yet that underinvestment itself, the cause of many of the government's shortcomings, is largely the responsibility of the Republican Party. The right has achieved an extraordinary trick of confidence destruction that has in turn primed many citizens, especially on the right, to believe any crazy thing about anything the government touches.

The most certain strategy to subvert the people's choice builds on this skepticism. It imagines certain swing states declaring, before Election Day, that they will cancel their popular election for president— or alternatively, that the legislature will vote at the end of Election Day for the slate of electors for the candidate whom the legislature believes reflects, in the words of that dangerous North Carolina law, "the will of the electorate."

Can they do this, legally?

Constitutionally, the answer is almost certainly yes. The Framers of our Constitution gave each state the power to "appoint" electors "in such Manner as the Legislature thereof may direct." Many legislatures exercised that power for much of the Republic's early history by picking the state's presidential electors directly themselves, without any popular vote at all. Those legislature-chosen electors then cast their ballot in the Electoral College, no doubt guided by the preferences of the legislature that picked them. Any legislature today that decided to pick electors directly would therefore have strong precedent to draw upon to justify its decision.

But could this happen today, politically?

A sober-minded observer would probably say that such a choice would be impossible—politically. How would the party controlling a legislature survive its next election if it told its people, "We don't trust you to vote"?

Yet here's where the rhetoric of democratic failure becomes so significant: a legislature that linked the cancellation of a presidential election to the perception that elections have been corrupted could, at least among the base of the party controlling the legislature, limit the political cost of that decision. "We've seen enough over the past years," its spokespeople might say, "to know that we can't trust our system of elections just now. There is too much unreliability in the process, too much fraud, too many 'illegals' trying to vote. We commit absolutely to creating a trustworthy system of elections. But right now, the corruption in our current system is just too great. Until we can fix that system, we must protect the electoral votes of our state from obvious political manipulation." With such rhetoric, a legislature might well lessen the political costs of canceling or nullifying the state's own presidential election. "We are a Republican state," the legislators would insist. "We will not allow fraud to deny a Republican victory."

And thus could the legislature—both constitutionally and politically—remove the people from the choice of their president.

Now before you get too outraged at this idea, recognize this: *Already, the vast majority of state legislatures have effectively rendered the votes of their voters irrelevant to the choice of president.* Almost every state today has a rule that makes presidential elections in their states essentially pointless. This is because of the system we've called "winner-take-all." Forty-eight states and the District of Columbia award presidential electors according to a winner-take-all method. That means that the winner of the popular vote in a state gets all the state's electoral votes—regardless of that proportion. In 1992 in Nevada, Bill Clinton received 37.4 percent of the popular vote, while George Bush received 34.7 percent and Ross Perot received 26.2 percent. Yet Bill Clinton received 100 percent of Nevada's electoral votes.[2]

In all but about ten swing states, the choice by the legislature to use winner-take-all is effectively a choice by the legislature—made long before Election Day—to make the voters in their states irrelevant in the presidential contest. No matter which way the political winds blow in any given election year, Kentucky is voting Red and New York is voting Blue. Thus, given the decision to allocate electors in a winner-take-all manner, do we really need an election in Kentucky? Or New York? In most states, elections under winner-take-all for all practical purposes become like Soviet show trials, with all the trappings of a genuine decision but no one doubting what the outcome will be.

One of us (Lessig) tried to mount a constitutional challenge to this (to him at least) obvious violation of equality among voters. Why should my vote in Massachusetts, he thought, not matter to the result in a presidential election when the vote of my nephew in Georgia does? But though one court of appeals judge, Judge Andrew Wynn, wrote a brilliant dissent, four courts of appeals upheld winner-take-all against the challenge.[3] Winner-take-all is constitutional in America, which means states are free to fool their citizens into believing that their vote matters, when anyone who knows anything about presidential politics knows that in most states it does not.

The upshot is startling: state legislatures are free to deny their people a meaningful role in selecting our president, either directly or indirectly. Directly, by canceling an election or by making the results merely advisory; indirectly, at least in solidly Red or Blue states, by adopting winner-take-all as the method for allocating electoral votes. Either way achieves the same result: removing the relevance of the vote of the people in their state on Election Day from the ultimate choice in allocating electors.

But the unique danger of a state legislature formally canceling an election is that it could happen in a critical swing state, not just a solidly Red or Blue state. If the state legislatures of Vermont and Wyoming canceled their respective state's presidential elections and appointed electors directly, it wouldn't make a difference in those states' electoral votes. Vermont always votes for the Democrat, and the Democratic state legislature in Vermont would surely appoint Democratic electors if it had the power to do so. The same is true of deeply Republican Wyoming. But swing states often split their vote for president and state legislature. Arizona, Georgia, Michigan, Pennsylvania, and Wisconsin all voted for President Biden in 2020. But each state also had a state legislature dominated by Republicans. If each of those Republican state legislatures had canceled its state's elections in 2020 and directly appointed Republican electors instead, Joe Biden would never have become president.

But is there any legal argument that might prevent a legislature from formally taking the vote away from its people?[4]

We're skeptical. We certainly wouldn't bet on the idea that the current originalist Supreme Court would limit a legislature's freedom to go back to 1789. But here are the strongest arguments that we believe could be made.

The first, ironically, builds on the decision the Court made in the Hamilton Electors' case, *Chiafalo v. Washington*. In that case, you'll remember, the question was whether electors were free to vote their conscience or whether a state had the power to direct them to vote as its legislature chose. The Court voted unanimously (though for different reasons) to uphold the states' power to control how electors vote. Even though no state had ever tried to exert such control until late in the twentieth century, the Court upheld that power because it was "the trust of a Nation that here, We the People rule."[5]

That "trust," however, would be betrayed by a legislature's decision to deny that "the People rule." If states could remove the people from the process of deciding who would govern them completely, then a key premise of our democracy would be destroyed—even if it's only a modern premise. Whatever the Framers imagined, our democratic culture has evolved. And the notion that partisans in a state legislature might deny the people a role in selecting our president could be deemed by the Court to no longer be allowable. Thus, the Supreme Court could declare that this power originally possessed by the states to ignore the will of its people had been lost by generations of disuse.

A second, doctrinally more rigorous constitutional claim may rest on the First Amendment. If the government decides to punish you based on your political views or affiliation, that could violate the Constitution. Not always: If you're the press secretary to the president and decide that you no longer support the president's party, it's not a First Amendment violation for the president to fire you. But the president can't retaliate against private citizens for opposing them. So, for example, the government can't impose a special tax on those who voted for the president's opponent. Similarly, if the majority party in a state legislature fears that most in the state would vote for an opposing party and in response removes their right to vote for president, that could raise an important First Amendment issue. Just as the government can't take away your money in retaliation for expressing your political views, so, too, it can't take away your right to vote because it fears you'll vote for a different party. The state legislature does not have the right to demand partisan loyalty. Nor should it have the power to punish the people for not being loyal.

We think that this argument might work—at least for us, but of course we're not Supreme Court justices. We don't think it has much chance of stopping a state legislature from trying to cancel its presidential election. That's because a state legislature planning to cancel an election would probably do so only at the last moment. It would make no sense for this strategy to be announced in January 2024, since in January, there is still time to solve whatever problems might be said to justify canceling an election. But on November 1, if a legislature declared that it was fearful of fraud and was therefore canceling its election, we fear that the courts would not move fast enough to block that decision. And if they did act fast enough, then the decision to invalidate the legislature's act would be a choice by the Court to disenfranchise the state completely because there would certainly be too little time to hold a whole new election after the Supreme Court rendered its decision—if federal law even permitted a state to hold one after Election Day. We think that the Court is unlikely to take that step.

We therefore think that this strategy, if deployed, is almost certain to work. But we also believe that in the near term the political costs of canceling the election in advance or gathering to vote on Election Day if the results go against the legislature's wishes make this strategy unlikely to be tried for now. It depends on how extreme or ruthless the state legislature is.

The stakes are even graver if we look further into the future. This step, once taken, leads us down a completely constitutional path toward permanent minority control of the presidency. The reason for that is because of partisan gerrymandering by state legislatures of their own districts. Although they are elected, state legislatures are not truly democratic institutions. Both political parties, but especially the Republican Party, have become ruthlessly effective at partisan gerrymandering. Powerful computer algorithms enable the party in control to draw district lines precisely so that it stays in control. As a result, a party that wins a minority of the statewide vote for legislators can win a supermajority in the legislature. In Wisconsin in 2018, Democrats won 53 percent of the votes for state legislators while Republicans won 45 percent. But extreme partisan gerrymandering gave the Republicans 63 seats, while Democrats won only 36. In a fair election, in which the number of seats won is proportional to the number of votes won, Democrats would have won 52 seats and Republicans 47. In this way, a minority party can entrench itself to control a state legislature indefinitely. Combined with the state legislature's power to appoint electors, the minority party could thus control the presidency.

There are few legal safeguards to prevent that future. In 2019, the Supreme Court decided in *Rucho v. Common Cause* that although partisan gerrymandering is "incompatible with democratic principles," federal courts cannot enforce any prohibition against it because the issue is a political question, and thus beyond the Court's jurisdiction. State constitutions are unlikely to provide enough protections to go beyond the federal Constitution. A few state supreme courts have held that their state constitutions prohibit partisan gerrymandering, but we doubt that many others will follow.

Some states use nonpartisan commissions to draw state legislative districts, which in theory should curb gerrymandering. But commissions that are established by the state legislature can be abolished by the state legislature. And if they are based on something other than a law passed by the legislature, they are in deep legal danger. In 2015, the Supreme Court upheld Arizona's redistricting commission, which had been created by the state's voters through a ballot initiative, in *Arizona State Legislature v. Arizona Independent Redistricting Commission.* But that case, too, is in mortal danger after *Moore v. Harper.* The Court decided the case 5–4, with Justice Ruth Bader Ginsburg writing the majority opinion and Chief Justice Roberts writing the dissent. Since then, Justice Ginsburg has been replaced by Justice Amy Coney Barrett, and Justice Anthony Kennedy, who also voted in the majority, has been replaced by Justice Brett Kavanaugh. Both new justices are likely to embrace at least the narrow version of the ISLT, and that version may well preclude a redistricting commission established by a ballot initiative.

As we noted in the last chapter, although the Supreme Court seemingly rejected even the weak form of ISLT that would have eliminated state constitutional limits on partisan gerrymandering, state supreme courts are at best deeply flawed institutions to protect the political process. Many states elect their supreme court justices, a practice that reintroduces all the pathologies of state elections into a judicial system that is supposed to safeguard them. Two states—South Carolina and Virginia—even empower the state legislature to appoint justices to their supreme courts. Suffice it to say that after *Rucho* federal courts will not save us from minority rule, and state supreme courts are at best an uncertain proposition to provide the protections that the Supreme Court has refused to provide.

If not courts, what might stop us from sliding into this dystopian pseudo-democracy? It is conceivable (if unlikely) that federal legislation could bar partisan gerrymandering of state legislative districts (the argument would rest on a correct but never-attempted reading of Congress's power under the Republican Guarantee Clause), thus preventing entrenched minority rule in state legislatures. But such legislation is highly unlikely to pass in the near term. The Senate rejected a ban on partisan gerrymandering of federal congressional districts (a context in which its constitutional footing is certain) in January 2022 when Republicans filibustered the election reform legislation advanced by Democrats. There is no reason to think that Republicans will have a change of heart on the measure, which they term a "federal takeover of state elections." Principled federalism and respect for state sovereignty aside, Republicans realize that they benefit from unconstrained partisan gerrymandering and will not willingly relinquish that advantage.

Even in a heavily gerrymandered state legislature, political constraints might still play a role. For a state legislature to seize the power to appoint presidential electors remains a stunningly antidemocratic power play. And though partisan gerrymandering can place a heavy thumb on the electoral scale, it can still be overcome by a sufficiently large majority. Perhaps enough Americans would be outraged at the affront to our democratic norms that they would look past their partisan preferences to oust a party that made such an extreme move. But partisan identities run deep, and though we hope that enough voters would give the highest priority to democracy itself, we confess that we cannot be certain they would. The polarized reaction to President Biden's description of the Trump wing of the Republican Party as "semi-fascist" because they deny the legitimate results of elections is not encouraging.[6]

One last line of defense is the elected officials' own commitment to democratic ideals and the rule of law. That commitment, if held, would prevent them from exploiting the vulnerabilities we have mapped in this chapter and the ones that precede it. But this book is premised on a profound skepticism about whether we can rely on politicians to keep faith with those principles. This nuclear strategy thus represents a profound threat to our democracy. It is the clearest and most dangerous path on our road map to a permanent minoritarian takeover.

---

tl;dr

The strategy: A state legislature cancels its election before Election Day and chooses the state's electors directly.

The chance that this strategy flips the results in 2025: very significant

The chance that this strategy flips results in future elections: very significant

Summary why: Legislatures directly appointed electors at the founding of the Republic and for many elections afterward. Only the political accountability of state legislators constrains this strategy. But extreme partisan gerrymandering enables a minority party to control a state legislature indefinitely, and neither state nor federal courts are likely to check that gerrymandering. The result is that a minority party can entrench itself in power in a state legislature and then seize for itself the appointment of presidential electors.

9

The Most Dangerous Strategy

A tweak on the plan described in the last chapter could be the easiest, and most potent, way to "steal an election." We hesitate to describe it because we see no way—absent the Supreme Court reversing itself—to avoid it in advance. The tweak does not require the legislature to cancel an election (which again would probably be constitutional, if politically costly) or appoint an alternative slate after Election Day (which again would not be constitutional). Instead, it depends upon a power the Supreme Court has already affirmed for state legislatures in *The Electors Cases:* to direct how electors may vote.

Recall the issue in *The Electors Cases:* did presidential electors have a right to vote contrary to how the state legislature had directed? The unanimous answer of the Supreme Court was "no": the state legislatures had the power to control how electors could vote. If electors violated that directive, they could be sanctioned, or even replaced. The Court did not hold that electors must vote as the people had voted: if a state had no law constraining electors, nothing in *The Electors Cases* would force electors to vote one way or the other. The issue in *The Electors Cases* was legislative power: did the electors have a constitutional right that constrains state legislatures? The United States Supreme Court said "no."

Building on that holding, the strategy in this chapter is this: The state legislature passes a law that directs that electors shall vote as the state legislature commands. By default, the law specifies that the electors shall vote in the Electoral College as the people have voted on Election Day. But the law reserves to the legislature the power to direct the electors to vote differently if it so chooses.

Let's spell this scenario out explicitly: Imagine that the North Carolina legislature directs that its electors in 2024 shall be the sixteen most senior members of the North Carolina National Guard. We might imagine that these people are nonpartisan or, more accurately, that they will accept the legislature's direction about how they must vote without much fuss. And imagine further that the law directs that those sixteen electors shall vote as the legislature specifies. The law presumptively requires that electors shall vote for the winner of the popular election as the state election board reports it. But imagine that it also reserves to the legislature a power to direct the electors to vote differently, by a resolution of the two houses of the North Carolina legislature, at any point before the Electoral College meets. Thus, the legislature could direct the electors to vote for a candidate other than the one the state election board reports as the winner. And it could require—as *Colorado Department of State v. Baca* affirms—that any elector not voting as the legislature directs be removed and replaced by an elector who will vote as the legislature directs. The legislature under this regime would retain the power to overrule the people's vote, by voting after Election Day to direct its electors to vote for someone other than the winner of the state's popular vote.

Applying that law, imagine that, after the election in 2024, many charge that the process in North Carolina was flawed. Two days before the Electoral College votes, the legislature passes a resolution directing the electors—again, all of whom were appointed on Election Day—to vote for the MAGA Republican candidate. On the day the Electoral College votes, the electors thus cast their ballots for the MAGA Republican. Any elector who violates that directive is automatically removed by the secretary of state and replaced with a MAGA Republican–supporting elector. The MAGA Republican thus wins North Carolina's electoral votes, the popular vote notwithstanding.

This is a presidential election, stolen—that is, if you believe that our Constitution has vested in "the People" the choice of their president *and* if the public voted contrary to how the legislature directs. This second condition could be difficult to know if the government of a state actively tries to conceal it by conjuring a cloud of confusion about the real results of the vote. But any legislature seeking to reserve the power to evade the vote of its citizens should prefer this strategy over the others we've described, because this strategy doesn't require that the legislature outright deny the people the right to vote. It only overrides the *apparent* result of their vote in cases where the election is plausibly said to have been marred by fraud. It could even be framed as a "democratic safety valve" designed to assure that a rogue, corrupted election does not frustrate the "true will" of the people. This strategy is deviously effective because it is both a theft in plain sight and a theft plausibly denied.

Could anything stop this democracy-defeating strategy?

Certainly, given the motivation behind the Court's decision in *The Electors Cases,* there is a principle that should defeat this strategy. Remember Justice Kagan's final words—"here, We the People rule." That's hardly an endorsement of a legislature's power to overrule the choice of its people. Yet the difficulty is that the opinion did nothing to cabin its reach to a legislature that was simply seeking to affirm— rather than overrule—the choice its people made for president. The Court simply assumed that legislatures would intend to ensure that the states' electors vote in accord with the people's choice. It assumed, in other words, that the legislature would only act in a prodemocratic way (just as it assumed, without any factual basis, that so-called faithless electors would only act in an antidemocratic way). But that assumption is not required by the rule the Court embraced, which simply gives the legislature the power to direct how its electors shall vote. And changing the rule to restrict the legislature's power to a power to echo the peoples' choice would require a new decision by the Court. It is difficult to imagine the Court handing down such a decision in the few weeks it would have to avoid this scenario. The best shot would be for the Court to allow any statute establishing this regime to be challenged immediately upon its passage. Such litigation would have to clear plenty of jurisdictional hurdles. Under existing doctrine, it's not clear that the Court would have the power to decide the case until it's almost too late.

We know that the Framers knew there was no perfect way to select the president. Even the Framers who supported direct election by the people realized that at the time, given the limits of communication, that was not feasible. But we also know that they were quite clear about the dangers in vesting the choice in state legislatures. Although the Framers allowed a state's legislature to *appoint* electors, none of them ever suggested that a legislature had the power to direct how the electors, once appointed—whether by the electorate or the legislature—would *cast* their ballots. Legislatures can act strategically; if they could decide who would get their state's vote, they could (and would) hold out for the candidate who promised their state the most or for the one with the most partisan support. By vesting the power to choose in a temporary body of electors—who must vote on the same day (in the days before Twitter or telephones, so with little opportunity to act strategically)—they thought they were minimizing the chance of intrigue. *The Electors Cases* have now defeated this central design feature, at least if a legislature is keen to subvert the popular vote. The Court should recognize this and find a way to correct it before it is too late.

What if the Supreme Court does not step in? Then all that remains in the defense of democracy is vigilance within the state. In the scenario we've outlined so far, the state legislature passes the law enabling this strategy before the election. But there's nothing stopping a state legislature from passing a law directing how its electors must vote at any time before the Electoral College votes, including after Election Day. No doubt the world would notice. But in the highly gerrymandered and partisan states that matter most, it's not clear that the world's noticing is enough. The people who planned January 6 knew the world would notice. They just didn't think that notice would matter enough to defeat their plans.

---

tl;dr

The strategy: State legislatures enact a law requiring the state's electors to cast their votes in the Electoral College as the legislature directs, regardless of the results of the election, at any time prior to the vote by the Electoral College

The chance that this strategy flips the results in 2025: very significant

The chance that this strategy flips results in future elections: very significant

Summary why: The law today clearly gives legislatures the power to direct how electors cast their ballot. We are confident that the Court did not intend this result and that, if given the chance, it would fix it. But it might not have that chance in time.

10

Fixing the Flaws in Presidential Democracy

We finished writing this book as America had reached an uncertain crossroads. Some of the flaws we've identified have been partially cured in the Electoral Count Reform Act of 2022. But that law, significant as it is, left some problems unsolved. We've written this book with the hope that a wider recognition of the threats might help build deeper support for even more reform.

These additional reforms are not rocket science. Each of the problems we've identified has a relatively clear solution. In this chapter, we'll map them. But we begin with a sobering acknowledgment.

This chapter proceeds on the assumption that changing the rules matters. Yet we acknowledge that it may well be that the critical flaw in our democracy today cannot be fixed by changing the rules. No rule change will cure a lack of good faith. The rickety and flawed Electoral Count Act never caused real trouble in its 135-year history because, until 2020, actors from both political parties sacrificed their own political gain for the good of the nation.

If good faith disappears, it's not clear that any system of rules can regulate the process perfectly. If each side comes to view the other as criminal or worse, each may feel entitled to do whatever it takes to assure its own victory—including ignoring the law completely.

We can't legislate good faith. We can only practice it. And we can only remark on how difficult it is to practice good faith in a world where the political media profits from rendering us less trusting and more outraged.

Nonetheless, we will map out the rule-based reforms that might address the problems we've identified. Although better rules cannot guarantee good faith, they can narrow the windows of opportunity for bad faith. Whether that's enough, history will tell.

1. Vice-Presidential Superpowers

We don't think that the vice president has any constitutionally compelled superpowers. As a result, we don't believe that anything needs to be done formally to address such powers. John Eastman's theory has been widely refuted, and very few now suggest anything approaching what he advocated. We now have a full and complete record of just why neither side—including Democrats, who now hold the vice presidency—should imagine that this path to subversion is open. There is nothing more to be done to close it, because this flaw has fixed itself.

That said, the constitutional framework the Founders gave us in the Twelfth Amendment is far from perfect. It says nothing explicitly about how Congress is supposed to resolve disputes about electoral votes. The Electoral Count Reform Act does an imperfect job of filling that gap, but statutes can always be repealed. And no one wants the constitutional crisis that would rage if Congress tried to ignore it in the heat of a disputed presidential election. Constitutional amendments are exceptionally hard to ratify, because absent a convention they require two-thirds of both the House and the Senate plus three-quarters of state legislatures to approve them. But in this case, it is both worth trying and might actually work. In time, it may be Democrats who try to exploit the electoral count for their own partisan gain. That alone should give Republicans reason to support a bipartisan and neutral constitutional amendment. Only partisans of chaos could want the legal framework to remain uncertain and vulnerable.

Constitutional amendments, however, are exceptionally hard to ratify. So we won't hold our breath.

2. Faithless Electors

The Supreme Court has cleared the way for states to remove any threat created by threatened or intimidated electors. We don't, again, believe that there was ever any real risk of bribery, which would just be too easy to uncover. But we do take seriously the potential that threats of violence may well drive an elector to vote contrary to their pledge—especially when an elector who is targeted by such threats can frame their vote as motivated by a public-regarding reason ("I'm acting like Sam Miles, supporting the candidate who won the popular vote!").

The simplest solution to this flaw would automatically substitute an elector if that elector voted contrary to his or her pledge. That was the rule in Colorado which the Supreme Court upheld in *Colorado Department of State v. Baca.* That rule could be adopted by all the states. We believe they should.

But there is a critical technical flaw in the system that must be addressed for this to work reliably. A system of automatic substitution needs to account for the one critical period when an elector voting for someone other than the candidate to whom they are pledged is actually constitutionally necessary. This is the case considered, but not covered, by the Twentieth Amendment.

Under the Twentieth Amendment, "If, at the time fixed for the beginning of the term of the President, the President-elect shall have died, the Vice President-elect shall become President." But what if the candidate to whom a majority of electors are pledged dies before the Electoral College votes? That person is not yet the "President-elect." Who then becomes president?

In this case, the Framers of the Twentieth Amendment imagined the electors exercising their discretion. As the Committee Report explained,

> A constitutional amendment is not necessary to provide for the case of the death of a party nominee before the November elections. Presidential electors and not the President are chosen at the November election. The electors, under the present Constitution *would be free* to choose a President, notwithstanding the death of a party nominee. Inasmuch as the electors *would be free* to choose a President, a constitutional amendment is not necessary to provide for the case of the death of a party nominee after the November elections and before the electors vote.[1]

But if electors don't have any legal discretion—if they are pledged to the dead candidate, and they are not free to vote for someone else—then their votes would be lost. And if enough votes for the winning party's candidate are lost like this, then that party could lose its majority in the Electoral College and trigger a contingent election in the House. That could then throw the presidency to the party that lost both the popular vote *and* the Electoral College.

Consider a hypothetical to make this point clear. Imagine that a candidate wins the popular vote on Election Day. Imagine that this victory secures to the candidate 280 electoral votes—10 more than necessary to prevail in the Electoral College. But imagine that the candidate then dies before the Electoral College votes. And finally, imagine that the vote of 20 of those 280 electors is controlled by state law, requiring the electors to vote as pledged and, if they don't so vote, requiring the secretaries of state to replace the "faithless" electors with electors who will vote as pledged. On the day the Electoral

College votes, those 20 electors vote for the candidate who has died. Even if the remaining 260 vote for the party's vice-presidential nominee, no candidate would achieve a majority in the Electoral College. Under the Twelfth Amendment, the decision is then passed to the House of Representatives. Imagine that the House votes on a party-line basis, and the candidate who lost the popular and (presumptive) electoral vote is then selected as president.

This possibility creates a very dangerous incentive: If this is the rule, then this is the one moment in the cycle of a presidential election when assassination could change control of the government, as opposed to simply passing the office to the politically aligned vice president.

This terrifying incentive needs to be eliminated. Unfortunately, though the Supreme Court glimpsed the problem in *Chiafalo*, it punted rather than resolving it. That leaves it to the states to express clearly that any statute purporting to bind electors is conditioned upon the candidate surviving until the Electoral College votes. If the candidate dies, then electors should have the freedom to vote as it makes sense to vote. That may mean voting for the vice-presidential candidate. But the better strategy would be to leave the choice to the electors' discretion, as the Framers of the Twentieth Amendment plainly presumed.

3. Rogue Governors

The Electoral Count Reform Act makes exploiting the governor's gambit significantly more difficult by subjecting the governor's certification to federal court review. The dynamics we've described in this book make it so that the new law does not—and arguably could not—completely neutralize the risk. Yet a few simple steps can strengthen the ECRA even further.

The recalcitrant governor's gambit works because the governor can defy a federal court's order and suffer the temporary penalties of criminal contempt, safe in the knowledge that the new president they help install will promptly pardon them upon taking office. But the president's pardon power is limited to *federal* offenses. The president has no power to pardon anyone for *state* crimes. So to deter a recalcitrant governor effectively, every state should pass a law making it a crime for the governor to defy any federal or state court's order about certifying the state's electors. (In many states, governors do not have carte blanche to pardon whomever they want for state crimes, so self-pardons would often be off the table.)

In addition to that change in state law, Congress can improve the ECRA itself to disarm more fully the recalcitrant governor's gambit, the vice president's sleight of hand, and the congressional override. The ECRA's chain of custody approach—attempting to ensure that the governor's certification is correct and then permitting Congress to consider only the governor's certificate—is fatally vulnerable if that chain isn't ironclad. If either the governor or the vice president substitutes a bogus slate of electors for the real ones, there is nothing that Congress can do but reject those bogus electors. Under the ECRA, it is procedurally impossible for Congress to consider the right slate instead. And that, as we explained, means that in a close election a recalcitrant rogue governor or the vice president can steal the election *even if Congress rejects the bogus slate* by depopulating the Electoral College.

The solution to this flaw is to add an additional ground for objection to the slate of electors the vice president opens: that a submission *other* than the one the vice president opens is the legitimate slate and that Congress should consider that legitimate slate instead. With that addition, it would still take a vote of both houses to sustain the objection, but the recalcitrant rogue governor's or the vice president's bogus slate is subject to at least *some* check.

Next, the ECRA retains the ECA's obscure and antiquated grounds for objection: that the electors were not "lawfully certified" and that the electors' votes were not "regularly given." As we saw in 2021, unscrupulous members of Congress can exploit that unclear text to raise improper objections that are actually about alleged fraud or misconduct in the state's popular vote. To make that more difficult, Congress should amend the ECRA to state the permissible grounds of objection more clearly. Those permissible grounds should be that a slate was not lawfully certified by the governor (to disarm the governor's gambit), that a slate other than the one opened by the vice president is the legitimate slate (to disarm the vice president's sleight of hand), and that an elector's vote was illegal (because it was cast for an ineligible candidate, because it was cast on the wrong day, because the elector themself was ineligible, or because it was the result of bribery or coercion). By listing the permissible grounds for objection more clearly, the law would make it absolutely obvious if a member raised an objection on an impermissible ground. Without some external check, such as a court, Congress might still accept an impermissible objection. But we hope that the obviousness of such lawless behavior would make the political price of doing so high enough that Congress wouldn't dare.

Finally, the ECRA should state more clearly what Congress really should be doing on January 6. The ECRA's chain of custody approach attempts first to ensure that the governor's slate complies with a federal court's decision about which slate is legitimate, and then to ensure that Congress counts the governor's court-approved slate. The point of this somewhat convoluted two-part rule is actually straightforward: to ensure that Congress counts the slate that a federal court has determined is the legitimate one. This is because courts, and not politicians, are the most trustworthy institution to make that determination. So the ECRA should simply say so. Putting that straightforward rule in the ECRA's text would make it clear what Congress's limited job is on January 6 and that there really cannot be any dispute about which slate was approved by the federal court's order. It's written in black and white.

With these improvements, we think the ECRA would be as strong as it could possibly be. But even then, it's not completely ironclad. In the end, we can hope to *minimize* the legal framework's reliance on the good faith of politicians and its vulnerability to manipulation by bad actors, but we cannot eliminate it entirely. Congress could still theoretically disobey the court's command, but at that point there's nothing more that written law can do.

4. The "Force Majeure" Game

Congress reformed the section 2 exception to Election Day. But there is much more to do. Its looseness was a strategic opportunity for inverting an election result, yet the new force majeure exception is dangerously unclear still. Congress must specify that only natural disasters, terrorist attacks, and similar catastrophic events are enough— not the force majeure of a lawyer-induced delay in determining the results or a demagogue's conspiracy theories of voter fraud. And it should require that a federal court determine whether the exception applies, not the state legislature. If it applies, then the law should assure that voting is completed. The *Succession* gambit should be blocked before the next election.

5. Who's the Judge?

Congress can do very little to constrain state legislatures from making themselves the judge of elections. The power to determine the "manner" of choosing electors is plainly vested by the Constitution in the states. One way for Congress to exert some influence is to leverage its power to determine the *time* when states choose electors. Congress may use this power to determine what, if anything, states may do after Election Day in the process of appointing their electors. It could specify that the naming of electors may be finalized after recounts, canvassing, and similar processes after Election Day—but only if these are performed by courts or nonpartisan election officials. That would rule out the state legislature setting itself up as the state's final canvassing board. We think that this could be a valid exercise of Congress's power to set the time for appointing electors, but it would be a challenging argument to make. It is quite possible that the Supreme Court would disagree and hold that it goes too far into the states' power to determine how electors are appointed.

The only clear political response is within the states themselves. Though state legislatures in key battleground states are wildly gerrymandered, we hope that there is still enough political will to keep these legislatures out of such an obviously vulnerable political position. We hope.

Alternatively, we believe work should be devoted to developing a judicial check on the political judging of electoral results, probably under the Due Process and Equal Protection Clauses of the Fourteenth Amendment. We're not convinced that it is possible—it's never been tried under state or federal constitutional law—but it should be tried.

6. The Nuclear and Most Dangerous Strategies

As with the previous threat, the federal government could do very little to block a state from canceling its own presidential election (the Nuclear Strategy) or a state legislature directing electors to vote however the legislature chooses (the Most Dangerous Strategy). The precedents are too clear or too new, and the federal power is too clearly constrained. At most, lawyers should be ready to press the obvious arguments for the Supreme Court to correct the corrupting incentive it has created. Just as it would be sensible to limit elector discretion to acts that advance democratic norms, it would make sense to limit the power of the legislature to control the vote of electors to rules that assure that "here, We the People rule."

There is also plenty to be done at the state level. Any legislature even contemplating such an action should feel the full force of citizen resistance. Early in the process, party leaders should be asked to commit on the record to permitting the people to vote, though in the world we're imagining—and warning against—it's not clear that such a commitment would have any real effect.

We hope that this resistance might also do more—specifically, that it would also press strongly to give more voters a voice in choosing the president. The Electoral College, determined by winner-take-all elections in almost every state, rendered more than 72 percent of the votes for president in 2020 irrelevant.[2] A movement to bind the states to respect the winner of the popular vote—the National Popular Vote Compact—is within striking distance of having enough states committed to trigger the compact and make the result in the Electoral College guaranteed to mirror the popular result nationally.[3] That single change would, overnight, render every voter in America equal. Even a simple proportional allocation of electors at the state level (if you get 43 percent of the vote, you get 43 percent of the electors), at least if all states adopted that strategy simultaneously, could make more voters more relevant. The current norm suppresses voter turnout in non-swing states. And it may well increase polarization: Why are Kentucky and West Virginia such solidly Red states? Why are Vermont and Massachusetts so clearly blue? Perhaps part of the reason comes from the absence of any other view ever being expressed in those states because the return from such spending is certain to be zero.

Each of the changes we propose could happen quickly. Not too quickly—we should be careful to avoid unintended consequences by giving many people the opportunity to game any potential solution. We know all too well that trying to hack the legal system can expose weaknesses that few imagined. But we have to try. And if Congress and states act, they will have successfully minimized the chance that the democratic results of a presidential election could be undermined.

11

The Soul of Democracy

In 1993, a conflict between the president of the Russian Federation, Boris Yeltsin, and the Russian Constitutional Court came to a head. For many months, the chief justice of the Russian Court had lectured and ordered and taunted the new Russian president. At one point, the Court declared a speech of the president unconstitutional. A speech! By October, Yeltsin had had enough. Tanks surrounded the Court—literally. The president ordered the court to shut down.

One of us (Lessig) was in Moscow when this happened. Shortly thereafter, he attended a meeting of court officials as they tried to work through what had just happened and what lessons were to be learned. One official, a lawyer, senior in the courts' bureaucracy, said he knew what had led the court to its craziness. "The rules allowed the court to meet whenever it wanted," he explained to the gathered foreign observers. "That led to terrible decisions by exhausted judges. If the rules were to specify only certain hours when judges could meet, then such decisions would not be made."

In the context of that moment, it seemed crazy to imagine that the outrageous interference in judicial independence the world had just seen could have been prevented by a simple change in opening times of the constitutional court. What Russia needed was a legal culture, a commitment to the rule of law and democracy that would be shared and practiced by everyone. That would have stopped Yeltsin. Tweaks to the rules don't produce a culture—or at least not overnight.

Both of us have wondered whether our own proposals for changes to the rules are just another example of such craziness. We can identify the rules changes that could make our democracy more robust and resilient. Chapter 10 did that. But unless good faith returns to this process, no simple change in the rules will be enough.

That's not an excuse to do nothing. Success may not be assured, but failure could be if we do not act. Doing nothing will only allow this culture of bad faith to normalize itself even more. We can't survive as a democracy if flat-out lies—whether by media talking heads or political leaders—flourish. Fixing rules is a first step. Fixing culture is the essential second step.

Even those fixes, however, would get us only so far. The risks we've written about are pressing and real. Yet in the broad scope of our history, they have never been consequential. As we've described, only twice, in 1876 and 2020, has the mechanism for reckoning the electoral vote ever threatened to derail a result. And only once has a presidential elector defected to the other side.

Yet as we've emphasized, there are features of our current system that defeat democracy—not episodically but always. Winner-take-all defeats democracy in every election: when all but two states give the winner of the popular vote all the electors from that state, that choice renders the vote of almost three-fourths of Americans completely irrelevant. Winner-take-all divides the nation into swing states and nonswing states, and no candidate in either party has any incentive to campaign in the nonswing states. That means that both candidates in both parties work extremely hard to woo voters in the ten or so swing states while ignoring voters in most of America. In effect, we have outsourced the choice of president to a small and unrepresentative segment of the country. In 2020, there were fourteen battleground states. Turnout was on average 4 points higher in those states. Ninety-eight percent of campaign visits were in those states. Among the fourteen, six were particularly important: Arizona, Florida, North Carolina, Ohio, Pennsylvania, and Wisconsin. Those six accounted for 84 percent of campaign spending and 71 percent of candidate appearances.[1] In 2024, there will be nine battleground states, and two battleground districts, together representing just 21 percent of America.[2] Thus a battle among a mere 21 percent of us will decide the winner of the next election. This is a problem not every twenty years or every 120 years. This is a problem every four years.

And this, of course, is just the beginning of a complete critique of the system of democracy that America has evolved: the way we fund campaigns, the way districts get drawn, the systems that make it harder for some to vote than for others, the filibuster in the Senate—each of these defeats the ideal of a representative democracy in which all count equally, not as grotesquely as a stolen election but, systematically, as effectively. We were raised to believe ours is the greatest democracy in the world. It is time we grow up and recognize just how flawed—and corrupted—that democracy has become. And then do something about it.

When Elena Kagan crafted her opinion rejecting the idea that electors are constitutionally free to vote their conscience, she took for granted that our nation embraced a democratic ideal. "Here," she told us at the end of her opinion, "We the People rule."

Yet that principle holds in America today only in our dreams. It is threatened by those who reject the constraints of truth. We should of course do what we can to protect against this most extreme violation of democratic norms. But we cannot take these steps without committing to much more extensive reform. Yes, obviously, democracy demands that elections not be stolen. But representative democracy demands much more than that. For now, we hope that shining a light on the catastrophic risk of a stolen presidential election can help the country prepare for—and, we hope, prevent—a cataclysmic attack on our democracy. For the future, we hope that success may inspire even more.

Our nation was born inspiring a world governed by monarchs and autocrats that representative democracy was possible. We could inspire again, if we could build the movement to finally realize representative democracy: as equal for all, and corrupted by none.

Notes

Chapter 1. A Coup in Search of a Legal Theory

1. In 2000, Democratic representatives sought to challenge the electoral college results, but no senator joined the objection, and Vice President Al Gore ruled the objection out of order. In 2004, California senator Barbara Boxer joined Ohio representative Stephanie Tubbs Jones to object to the counting of the Ohio electoral votes. Both acknowledged that their only purpose was to force a debate on "flawed voting practices." They expressly stated that they did not want or intend to reverse the results of the election. Maura Reynolds, *Boxer Poses a Challenge, Briefly*, L.A. TIMES (Jan. 7, 2005, 12:00 AM), https://www.latimes.com/archives/la-xpm-2005-jan -07-na-electoral7-story.html [perma.cc/3DH6-GX5D].

2. Russell Berman, *Kamala Harris Might Have to Stop the Steal*, ATLANTIC (Oct. 6, 2021), https://www.theatlantic.com/politics/archive/2021/10/kamala-harris -trump-january-6/620310/ [perma.cc/UL89-CEXT].

Chapter 2. The Scenario

1. *Florida Ballots Project*, National Opinion Research Center at the U. of Chi., http://web.archive.org/web/20080724084023/http:/www2.norc.org/fl [perma .cc/NBR2-LVB5].

2. *User Clip: Al Gore Concession Speech after Supreme Court Decision*, C-SPAN (Nov. 20, 2020), https://www.c-span.org/video/?c4924717/user-clip-al-gore-concession -speech-supreme-court-decision [perma.cc/RP5J-HVKG].

3. Jan Zilinsky et al., *Which Republicans Are Most Likely to Think the Election Was Stolen? Those Who Dislike Democrats and Don't Mind White Nationalists*, WASH. POST (Jan. 19, 2021, 5:07 PM), https://www.washingtonpost.com/politics/2021/01/19 /which-republicans-think-election-was-stolen-those-who-hate-democrats-dont -mind-white-nationalists/ [perma.cc/CYK2–86P8].

4. *Case Tracker*, Election L. Prog. at Ohio St. Univ. Moritz Coll. of L., https://

electioncases.osu.edu/case-tracker/?sortby=filing_date_desc&keywords=&status=all&state=all&topic=25 [perma.cc/WCC8-8BVL].

5. For a comprehensive review of polling, see Alison Durkee, *Americans Still Blame Trump for the Insurrection—And Think Democracy Is under Threat, Polls Find*, FORBES (Jan. 3, 2022, 12:26 PM), https://www.forbes.com/sites/alisondurkee/2022/01/03/americans-still-blame-trump-for-january-6-insurrection-and-think-democracy-is-under-threat-polls-find/?sh=539c10017989 [perma.cc/X2ZD-SABU].

6. Monmouth University Poll, *National: Most Say Fundamental Rights under Threat* (June 20, 2023) (press release), https://www.monmouth.edu/polling-institute/documents/monmouthpoll_us_062023.pdf/.

7. Aaron Blake, *"What's the Downside for Humoring Him?": A GOP Official's Unintentionally Revealing Quote about the Trump Era*, WASH. POST (Nov. 10, 2020, 10:15 AM), https://www.washingtonpost.com/politics/2020/11/10/whats-downside-humoring-him-gop-officials-unintentionally-revealing-quote-about-trump-era/ [perma.cc/5MWH-T52L] [perma.cc/2PK2-BZ24].

8. Alicia M. Cohn, *Trump Calls for Revolution, Blasts Electoral College*, HILL (Nov. 7, 2012), https://thehill.com/blogs/twitter-room/other-news/133889-trump-calls-for-revolution-blasts-electoral-college [perma.cc/WU27-CQHD].

9. Richard Winger, *2022 Election Returns Suggest Electoral College Could Damage Republicans in 2024*, 38 BALLOT ACCESS NEWS 1 (Dec. 2022).

Chapter 3. VP Superpowers

1. Matthew A. Seligman, *John Eastman Is Right: His Election Memo Was "Crazy,"* SLATE (Oct. 22, 2021, 1:21 PM), https://slate.com/news-and-politics/2021/10/john-eastman-crazy-election-memo-trump.html [perma.cc/HQT2-B6FS].

2. Robin Lindley, *Trump and His 3,500 Suits: Prosecutor and Author Reveals in Interview His Portrait of "Plaintiff in Chief,"* ABA J. (Apr. 20, 2022, 8:49 AM CDT), https://www.abajournal.com/web/article/attorney-and-author-on-his-portrait-of-donald-trump-through-more-than-3500-lawsuits [perma.cc/UPQ7-HEYY]; Kate Sullivan et al., *Trump Threatens to Sue Top Democrats Adam Schiff and Nancy Pelosi amid Impeachment Inquiry*, CNN POLITICS (Oct. 12, 2019, 10:00 PM), https://www.cnn.com/2019/10/12/politics/trump-threatens-sue-schiff-pelosi/index.html [perma.cc/LZ9X-Q9PB]; Guardian US Staff, *The Long List of Legal Cases against Donald Trump*, GUARDIAN (Feb. 7, 2022, 2:00 AM), https://www.theguardian.com/us-news/ng-interactive/2022/feb/07/donald-trump-list-legal-cases [perma.cc/8HKT-T986]; Josh Marcus & Louise Hall, *Here Are All 29 Lawsuits Trump Is Facing Now That He Has Left Office*, INDEPENDENT (May 19, 2021, 3:45 PM), https://finance.yahoo.com

/news/lawsuits-trump-facing-now-left-222753636.html [perma.cc/4GET-RLGF]; David A. Fahrenthold et al., *Trump Faces an Onslaught of Legal Problems, as Investigations and Dozens of Lawsuits Trail Him from Washington to Florida,* WASH. POST (Mar. 20, 2021, 1:12 PM), https://www.washingtonpost.com/politics/trump-investi gations-lawsuits/2021/03/17/1ca3806c-8379-11eb-81db-b02f0398f49a_story.html [perma.cc/N3XT-9LE3]; Nick Penzenstadler & Susan Page, *Exclusive: Trump's 3,500 Lawsuits Unprecedented for a Presidential Nominee,* USA TODAY (June 1, 2016, 1:24 PM), https://www.usatoday.com/story/news/politics/elections/2016/06/01/donald -trump-lawsuits-legal-battles/84995854/ [perma.cc/JBY3-ECLJ].

3. Days before January 6, Representative Louis Gohmert filed an unsuccessful lawsuit asking the courts to declare Eastman's theory correct. The trial court dismissed the case because Gohmert had no legal standing to bring the case, and the Supreme Court never ruled on the issue.

4. It is worth pausing here to explain why counting necessarily involves some minimal level of substantive determination of the validity of the electoral votes. It's reasonable to think that counting should be a purely arithmetic task, and nothing more. But imagine that Congress receives two pieces of paper, each of which says: "These are the electoral votes for the Commonwealth of Pennsylvania." Both bear what appears to be the signature of the governor. But the two pieces of paper claim that the state's electoral votes were cast for different candidates. It is clear that one submission is genuine, and the other is a forgery. In order to count Pennsylvania's electoral votes, Congress has to decide which is which. In today's world of modern communications, resolving that dispute is trivially easy—but Congress must resolve it just the same. The real question, as we will explore in later chapters, is *which* disputes Congress has the power to resolve.

5. John Eastman, *Privileged and Confidential: January 6 Scenario* (unpublished memo), *available at* https://www.documentcloud.org/documents/21066248-eastman -memo.

6. *See* David Fontana & Bruce Ackerman, *Thomas Jefferson Counts Himself into the Presidency,* 90 VA. L. REV. 551 (2004).

7. *Supra.* See also Edward B. Foley, *Preparing for a Disputed Presidential Election: An Exercise in Election Risk Assessment and Management,* 51 LOY. U. CHI. L. J. 309, 326 (2020).

8. The certificate was to list the number of votes each candidate received—e.g., Votes for Jefferson: 4; Votes for Burr: 4, etc.—but instead listed the votes of each elector separately.

9. At least eventually, because Jefferson actually tied with Aaron Burr in the

Electoral College. Jefferson's party intended Jefferson as its presidential candidate and Burr as its vice-presidential candidate. But in 1800, four years before ratification of the Twelfth Amendment, electors couldn't cast votes for president and vice president separately. Instead, the presidency was awarded to the candidate with the most electoral votes and the vice presidency was awarded to the candidate with the second-most votes. That rule made sense to the Framers of the original Constitution, who didn't anticipate the rise of political parties and party tickets. In 1800 it meant that the House of Representatives, voting by delegation with each state having a single vote, got to award the presidency to one of the top three candidates. In 1804, the Twelfth Amendment replaced that broken system with the one we have today— each elector casts a vote for president and a vote for vice president.

10. The newspapers made three accusations. First, they charged that the law Vermont passed in 1791 establishing a "Grand Committee" of the governor and legislators to select the electors had expired after the 1792 election. But it hadn't. Second, they charged that the electors were invalidly selected by a mere "resolve" rather than by regular legislation. But a "resolve" by the Grand Committee was the method the legislature had chosen in the 1791 legislation. Third, they charged that Vermont had selected its electors outside the 34-day window mandated by federal law. But they picked the electors right on time.

11. *See* State of Missouri Certificate of Votes for President and Vice President, 2020, NAT'L ARCHIVES (Dec. 14, 2020), https://www.archives.gov/files/electoral -college/2020/vote-missouri.pdf [perma.cc/K322-AFM8]; State of Missouri Certificate of Votes for President and Vice President, 2016, NAT'L ARCHIVES (Dec. 19, 2016), https://www.archives.gov/files/electoral-college/2016/vote-missouri.pdf (2016) [perma.cc/95LP-HG2K]. We are grateful to Michael Rosin for pointing this out to us.

12. Lawrence Lessig, *Another Way to Elect a President: The VP's Role,* at 12:50– 13:47 (Nov. 2, 2020) (podcast), https://equalcitizens.us/another-way-to-elect-a-pres ident-the-vps-role-part-9/ [perma.cc/78CS-7NTB].

13. Matthew A. Seligman, *The Vice President's Non-Existent Unilateral Power to Reject Electoral Votes* 9 (Jan. 6, 2022) (unpublished draft), https://papers.ssrn.com /sol3/papers.cfm?abstract_id=3939020 [perma.cc/LQA5-FR5L]. Seligman testified in the California Bar's misconduct proceeding against John Eastman. You can read his testimony at https://papers.ssrn.com/sol3/papers.cfm?abstract_id=4552179 [perma.cc /4VCP-T2EU].

14. Brief for the Defendant at Ex. N., Eastman v. Thompson, No. 8:22-cv-00099 (C.D. Cal. Mar. 2, 2022).

15. Daniel W. Tuttle Jr., *The 1960 Election in Hawaii*, 14 W. Pol. Q. 331, 337 (Mar. 1961).

16. A few of the Trump electors refused to go along with the plot. They were replaced in the "alternative" submissions with other Trump loyalists.

17. See the exhaustive report at Ryan Goodman, *Timeline: False Alternate Slate of Electors Scheme, Donald Trump and His Close Associates,* Just Sec. (July 18, 2022), https://www.justsecurity.org/81939/timeline-false-alternate-slate-of-electors-scheme -donald-trump-and-his-close-associates/ [perma.cc/2AHX-KTY2].

Chapter 4. "Faithless" Electors

1. Marina McIntyre, *Donald Trump Launches Twitter Tirade over Barack Obama's Victory,* Guardian (Nov. 7, 2012, 02:45 PM), https://www.theguardian.com/world /2012/nov/07/donald-trump-twitter-tirade-obama [perma.cc/4LAZ-HT25].

2. *Donald Trump's New York Times Interview: Full Transcript,* N.Y. Times (Nov. 23, 2016), https://www.nytimes.com/2016/11/23/us/politics/trump-new-york-times -interview-transcript.html [perma.cc/A6BU-SUSS].

3. The electors were targeting 37 because they expected Trump's margin would be 74. In the end it was 77.

4. Republican Share of Congress by State (unpublished) [perma.cc/P8ER -Q62Y].

5. The Federalist No. 68 (Alexander Hamilton).

6. Robert M. Alexander, Representation and the Electoral College 148 (2019).

7. Statement of Elbridge Gerry, May 31, 1787, in Gaillard Hunt & James Brown Scott, Eds., The Debates in the Federal Convention of 1787, which Framed the Constitution of the United States of America, reported by James Madison . . . (1920), *available at* https://avalon.law.yale.edu /18th_century/debates_531.asp.

8. Alexander Keyssar, Why Do We Still Have the Electoral College? 33 (2020).

9. Michael L. Rosin believes the history to be fuzzier but agrees that no elector flipped to supporting the "principal opponent." See Michael L. Rosin, *A History of Elector Discretion,* 41 N. Ill. U. L. Rev. 125 (2020), https://huskiecommons.lib.niu .edu/niulr/vol41/iss1/1/ [perma.cc/XK2X-DFAH]; Michael L. Rosin, *A History of Elector Discretion—Part Two,* 41 N. Ill. U. L. Rev. 1 (2021), https://huskiecommons .lib.niu.edu/niulr/vol41/iss2/2/ [perma.cc/29WR-JU92].

10. Mike Rappaport, *The Originalist Disaster in* Chiafalo, L. & LIBERTY (Aug. 7, 2020), https://lawliberty.org/the-originalist-disaster-in-chiafalo/ [perma.cc/8FE8 -NZFM].

11. Chiafalo v. Washington, 140 S. Ct. 2316, 2328 (2020).

12. Richard L. Hasen, *The Coming Reckoning over the Electoral College,* SLATE (Sept. 4, 2019, 11:08 AM), https://slate.com/news-and-politics/2019/09/electoral -college-supreme-court-lessig-faithless-electors.html [perma.cc/3G7Q-Q99A].

13. The current law is N.C. Gen. Stat. § 163–212 (2020).

Chapter 5. Rogue Governors

1. That's true for Florida, Louisiana, and South Carolina. In Oregon, there was a question about whether a single elector was constitutionally eligible to serve because he had also been a postmaster for the federal government.

2. Bradley applied the same principle to the disputed vote from Oregon. The issue there wasn't allegations of fraud, but rather who got to appoint the replacement elector if the original elector was constitutionally ineligible. As with the three other states, Bradley decided that the legitimate elector was the one appointed pursuant to Oregon's law.

3. Rand Paul (@RandPaul), TWITTER (Jan. 6, 2021, 4:46 PM), https://twitter .com/RandPaul/status/1346936083351793665?ref_src=twsrc%5Etfw [perma.cc/73ES -CNA8].

4. *Mitch McConnell Senate Speech Transcript January 6: Rejects Efforts to Overturn Presidential Election Results,* REV (Jan. 6, 2021), https://www.rev.com/blog/tran scripts/mitch-mcconnell-senate-speech-on-election-confirmation-transcript-january-6 [perma.cc/KUZ7-XATK].

5. The embarrassing inconsistency at the core of *Bush v. Gore,* 531 U.S. 98 (2000), in at least the position of Chief Justice Rehnquist and Justices Scalia and Thomas, is this: They all said that the determinative factor in interpreting Florida law was the text of the Florida statutes. But they all also insisted that the Florida legislatures placed completing their count by the "safe harbor" deadline above all other interests—including assuring that all votes get counted. Yet the source of that latter, and determinative, judgment was not the text of any statute. It was the interpretation of this text, by these three federal judges. That precisely was what they had criticized the Florida Supreme Court for doing—even though principles of federalism would certainly prefer that Florida judges interpret Florida law rather than federal judges.

6. 167 Cong. Rec. 55–56 (2021).

7. McLinko v. Dep't of State, 279 A.3d 539, 582 (Pa. 2022).

8. A distinguished group of conservatives, including two former Republican senators and three prominent former federal judges appointed by Republican presidents (including Judge Luttig, whom we met in Chapter 2), authored a detailed report offering the "conservative case that Trump lost and Biden won the 2020 presidential election." Their report left no room for doubt: "Our conclusion is unequivocal: Joe Biden was the choice of a majority of the Electors, who themselves were the choice of the majority of voters in their states." See Lost, Not Stolen, https://lostnotstolen.org [perma.cc/LFN9-Y5VA].

9. Jack Arnholz, *Sen. Rand Paul Continues Making False Claims of 2020 Election Fraud,* ABC News (Jan. 24, 2021), https://abcnews.go.com/Politics/sen-rand-paul-continues-making-false-claims-2020/story?id=75446712 [perma.cc/Z3GJ-YRR5].

10. Stephen A. Siegel, *The Conscientious Congressman's Guide to the Electoral Count Act of 1887,* 56 Fla. L. Rev. 541, 620–24 (2004) ("Finding a vote to be 'lawfully certified' encompasses additional grounds for rightful rejection: that the governor issued his section 3 certificate to electors who were not entitled to it under state law; or that state election officials had acted fraudulently.").

Chapter 6. The "Force Majeure" Game

1. There have been four other times over the last century when both Senate seats from a state flipped parties in the same year: Tennessee in 1994, Minnesota in 1978, Kentucky in 1956, and Indiana in 1916.

2. Act of Mar. 1, 1792, ch. 8, § 1, 1 Stat. 239.

3. Michael T. Morley, *Postponing Federal Elections due to Election Emergencies,* 77 Wash. & Lee L. Rev. Online 179, 184 (2020).

4. Edward B. Foley, Presidential Elections and Majority Rule: The Rise, Decline, and Potential Restoration of the Jeffersonian Electoral College (2020).

5. Cong. Globe, 28th Cong., 2nd Sess., 21 (statement of Rep. Duncan).

6. Alexander Keyssar, Why Do We Still Have the Electoral College? 32–33 (2020).

7. Joshua Matz, email to Lawrence Lessig, Jan. 20, 2022 (on file with authors).

8. Michael T. Morley, *Postponing Federal Elections due to Election Emergencies,* 77 Wash. & Lee L. Rev. Online 179, 188 (2020).

9. Michael L. Rosin, *What Did the Twenty-Eight Congress Mean by a "Failed*

Election?," *available at* https://papers.ssrn.com/sol3/papers.cfm?abstract_id=4339759 [perma.cc/KRE5-SNBV].

10. Bostock v. Clayton County, 140 S. Ct. 1731 (2020).

11. Joshua Matz, *The Plain Meaning of Title VII, Take Care,* July 8, 2019, *available at* https://takecareblog.com/blog/the-plain-meaning-of-title-vii [perma.cc/8HL8 -83LF].

12. N.C. Gen. Stat. Ann. § 163–213(a).

13. Tex. Const. art. IV, § 8.

Chapter 7. Who's the Judge?

1. Martin Pengelly, *Trump Call to "Find" Votes Was Threat to My Safety, Georgia Elections Official Says,* GUARDIAN (Nov. 2, 2021), https://www.theguardian.com /us-news/2021/nov/02/trump-georgia-elections-official-brad-raffensperger [perma.cc /AH62-JMHN].

2. Josh Marshall, *Trump Demands Supporters Cheat in 2022 and 2024 Elections,* TALKING POINTS MEMO (Jan. 19, 2022, 11:57 AM), https://talkingpointsmemo.com /edblog/trump-demands-supporters-cheat-in-2022-and-2024-elections [perma.cc /6BGA-7JCU].

3. Tex. Elec. Code § 221.002(e).

4. In light of the results in 2020, it is astonishing that the Court treated the "safe harbor" date as sacrosanct. In 2020, Wisconsin didn't complete its review of its results until after the safe harbor day. Its votes were nonetheless counted without incident.

5. Vikram David Amar & Akhil Reed Amar, *Eradicating Bush-League Arguments Root and Branch: The Article II Independent State-Legislature Notion and Related Rubbish,* 2021 SUP. CT. REV. 1 (2022).

6. 21-1271 Moore v. Harper (06/27/2023), https://www.supremecourt.gov/opin ions/22pdf/21-1271_3f14.pdf [perma.cc/C5F2-BF3F].

7. Akhil Reed Amar, *Bush, Gore, Florida, and the Constitution,* 61 FLA. L. REV. 945, 958–60, n.49 (2009).

Chapter 8. The Nuclear Option

1. *See Voting Laws Roundup: December 2021,* BRENNAN CTR. FOR JUST. (Jan. 12, 2022), https://www.brennancenter.org/our-work/research-reports/voting-laws -roundup-december-2021 [perma.cc/VX22-LHGR] ("More than 440 bills with pro- visions that restrict voting access have been introduced in 49 states in the 2021 legis-

lative sessions. These numbers are extraordinary: state legislatures enacted far more restrictive voting laws in 2021 than in any year since the Brennan Center began tracking voting legislation in 2011. More than a third of all restrictive voting laws enacted since then were passed this year."). Predictions of actual results are complicated by the fact that additional barriers to voting could hurt Republicans by dampening turnout among white voters without a college degree. *See, e.g.*, Robert Griffin, *Republicans Want to Make It Much Harder to Vote; That Strategy Could Backfire*, WASH. POST (Mar. 22, 2021, 9:33 AM), https://www.washingtonpost.com/outlook/2021/03 /22/republican-vote-restriction-turnout/?case=fms [perma.cc/M5H4-LWFS]. For more on the complicated interaction between absolute turnout and partisan advantage, see Lori Robertson, *Sanders' Shaky Turnout Claim*, FACTCHECK.ORG (Jan. 12, 2022), https://www.factcheck.org/2016/06/sanders-shaky-turnout-claim/ [perma.ccQUT8 -GDFW].

There is a wealth of evidence that strict voter ID laws disproportionately impact voters of color. *See, e.g.*, Zoltan Hajnal, John Kuk & Nazita Lajevardi, *A Disproportionate Burden: Strict Voter Identification Laws and Minority Turnout*, 10 POLITICS, GROUPS, AND IDENTITIES 126 (June 2020) (using nationwide county-level turnout data to demonstrate a race-based gap in turnout in states with strict voter ID laws); Bernard L. Fraga & Michael G. Miller, *Who Do Voter ID Laws Keep from Voting*, 84 J. POL. 1091 (Apr. 2022) (arguing that its "strict identification laws will stop a disproportionately minority, otherwise willing set of registered voters from voting," in part based on a finding that voters in Texas who would be barred from voting are disproportionately Black and Latino); Justin Grimmer and Jesse Yoder, *The Durable Differential Deterrent Effects of Strict Photo Identification Laws*, 10 POL. SCI. RESEARCH & METHODS 453 (July 2022) (demonstrating, based on the case of North Carolina, that voter identification laws' negative effect on turnout persists even after they are repealed). *See generally The Impact of Voter Suppression on Communities of Color*, BRENNAN CTR. FOR JUST. (Jan. 10, 2022), https://www.brennancenter.org/our-work /research-reports/impact-voter-suppression-communities-color [perma.cc/2KQ-DA7C] (collecting these studies and a couple more).

Eight bills imposing harsher voter ID requirements have been enacted in seven states since the 2020 election. *Voting Laws Roundup, supra* (AR H.B. 1112, AR H.B. 1244, FL S.B. 90, GA S.B. 202, MT S.B. 169, NH H.B. 523, TX S.B. 1, WY H.B. 75).

Another thirteen bills in six other states would either impose a new or stricter ID requirement for mail voting (such as providing a driver's license number or partial Social Security number to apply for or return mail ballots), implement new or stricter voter ID requirements for in-person voting, or both. *Voting Laws Roundup: May 2021*, BRENNAN CTR. FOR JUST. (May 26, 2022), https://www.brennancenter.org /our-work/research-reports/voting-laws-roundup-may-2022?_ga=2.125053194 .1423488210.1660665220-195869934.1655954670 [perma.cc/7RQ4-LL3L] (AZ H.B. 2289, AZ H.C.R. 2025, IA H.F. 2526, IA S.F. 2343, MI S.B. 285, MO H.B. 1878, NH H.B. 1542, NH S.B. 418, NY A.B. 9125, PA H.B. 1800, PA H.J.R. 1596, PA S.J.R. 106, PA S.J.R. 735).

Voters of color also consistently face longer wait times on Election Day. These longer wait times and the number of voters they discourage would be exacerbated by cutting alternative options, such as vote-by-mail or early voting. *See, e.g.,* Hannah Klain, Kevin Morris, Max Feldman & Rebecca Ayala, *Waiting to Vote,* BRENNAN CTR. FOR JUST. (June 3, 2020), https://www.brennancenter.org/sites/default/files/2020-06 /6_02_WaitingtoVote_FINAL.pdf [perma.cc/6AQY-QE7F]; M. Keith Chen, Kareem Haggag, Devin G. Pope & Ryne Rohla, *Racial Disparities in Voting Wait Times: Evidence from Smartphone Data* (Nat'l Bureau of Econ. Rsch., Working Paper No. 26487, 2020), https://www.nber.org/system/files/working_papers/w26487/w26487.pdf [perma.cc/7EKB-FMQ8]; David Cottrell, Michael C. Herron & Daniel A. Smith, *Voting Lines, Equal Treatment, and Early Voting Check-In Times in Florida,* 21 ST. POL. & POL'Y Q. 109 (June 2021). *See generally The Impact of Voter Suppression on Communities of Color, supra* (collecting these studies and more).

Many of the new Republican-backed voting restrictions cut these alternative options. *See generally Voting Laws Roundup: December 2021,* BRENNAN CTR. FOR JUST. (Jan. 12, 2022), https://www.brennancenter.org/our-work/research-reports/voting -laws-roundup-december-2021 [perma.cc/VX22-LHGR] (collecting all of the new restrictive voting laws in a table sorted by their effects on voting).

For similar reasons (among others like inferior transportation access), polling place consolidation is also especially harmful for the turnout of racial and ethnic minorities. *See, e.g.,* Enrico Cantoni, *A Precinct Too Far: Turnout and Voting Costs,* 12 AM. ECON. J.: APPLIED ECON. 61 (Jan. 2020); Kevin Morris & Peter Miller, *Voting in a Pandemic: COVID-19 and Primary Turnout in Milwaukee, Wisconsin,* 58 URB. AFFAIRS REV. 597 (Mar. 2022). *See generally The Impact of Voter Suppression on Communities of Color,* BRENNAN CTR. FOR JUST. (Jan. 10, 2022), https://www.brennan center.org/our-work/research-reports/impact-voter-suppression-communities-color [perma.cc/2PKQ-DA7C].

Three bills in three states reduce polling place availability (locations or hours).

Voting Laws Roundup: December 2021, Brennan Ctr. for Just. (Jan. 12, 2022), https://www.brennancenter.org/our-work/research-reports/voting-laws-roundup -december-2021 [perma.cc/VX22-LHGR] (listing IA S.F. 413, MT S.B. 196, TX S.B. 1 as restrictive voting legislation that reduces polling place availability).

2. Fed. Election Commission, Federal Elections 92: Election Results for the U.S. President, the U.S. Senate and the U.S. House of Representatives, FEC (1993), fec.gov/resources/cms-content/documents/federalelections92.pdf [perma.cc/M9TM -N98Q].

3. Baten v. McMaster, 967 F.3d 345, 361–80 (4th Cir. 2020), as amended (July 27, 2020) (Wynn, J., dissenting).

4. The best argument may be Mark Bohnhorst, Michael Fitzgerald & Aviam Soifer, *Gaping Gaps in the History of the Independent State Legislature Doctrine:* Mc-Pherson v. Blacker, *Usurpation, and the Right of the People to Choose Their President* (Dec. 7, 2022), https://ssrn.com/abstract=4296483 [perma.cc/27DQ-JVHY].

5. Chiafalo v. Washington, 140 S. Ct. 2316, 2328 (2020).

6. Christopher Cadelago & Olivia Olander, *Biden Calls Trump's Philosophy "Semi-Fascism,"* Politico (Aug. 25, 2022, 06:45 PM), https://www.politico.com/news /2022/08/25/biden-trump-philosophy-semi-fascism-00053831 [perma.cc/3VV4-G5EC].

Chapter 10. Fixing the Flaws in Presidential Democracy

1. Brief of Michael L. Rosin et al., as Amici Curiae, pp. 19–20, Chiafalo v. Washington, 140 S. Ct. 2316 (2020).

2. David Wasserman et al., *2020 National Popular Vote Tracker,* Cook Pol. Rep. (Nov. 2020), https://www.cookpolitical.com/2020-national-popular-vote-tracker [perma.cc/G8M3-88S2]; Politico Staff, *The 8 States Where 2020 Will Be Won or Lost: A Politico Deep Dive,* Politico (Sept. 8, 2020, 4:30 AM), https://www.politico .com/news/2020/09/08/swing-states-2020-presidential-election-409000 [perma.cc /6NGV-UEN7]; *Presidential Results,* CNN Politics (last updated Mar. 8, 2021), https://www.cnn.com/election/2020/results/president#mapfilter=keyrace [perma.cc /YD5T-S9CL].

3. The National Popular Vote Compact is an agreement among states that when states representing 270 electoral votes concur, the member states will select the slate of electors representing the winner of the popular vote, thereby guaranteeing that candidate becomes president. See *Agreement among the States to Elect the President by National Popular Vote,* Nat'l Popular Vote, https://www.nationalpopularvote.com /written-explanation [perma.cc/2GXZ-78S2].

Chapter 11. The Soul of Democracy

1. *America Goes to the Polls 2020,* Nonprofit Vote 24 (Mar. 18, 2021), https://www.nonprofitvote.org/wp-content/uploads/2021/03/america-goes-polls-2020–7.pdf [perma.cc/H56T-DXD5].

2. *There Will Be Only Nine Battleground States in 2024 Presidential Election* (Nov. 15, 2022), https://perma.cc/9PEB-9EV5].

Index